Introduction

Eugene Eric Kim

Browse any bookstore, and you'll find scores of Java books on the shelves. Pick up any magazine or newspaper—technical or otherwise—and you'll likely find some mention of Java. With all the fuss these days, it would be nice if someone answered a simple question or two.

What the heck is Java, and why should you care?

The answer is not straightforward, especially because the word "Java" can mean so many things. Java is an object-oriented language that's simpler than C++, but many languages can make that claim. Java uses a virtual machine for portability, but so do cross-platform compilers that generate native, high-performance binaries. Java means coffee, but programmers prefer caffeine in carbonated form.

The hard truth is that most of the principles behind Java aren't new, and many past technologies based on similar principles have failed. What makes Java different from these past technologies is that both industry and current technology are conducive to accepting and implementing these old/new principles. The widespread use of a global network, the new emphasis on interoperability and open standards, the existence of high-performance machines and standard component models, all of these are reasons we now embrace Java. Java was simply at the right place at the right time.

Many facets of Java are often overlooked in today's literature, most likely because of its all-encompassing nature. Too many books focus entirely on the syntax of the language, providing neither breadth nor context for properly understanding how and why Java is useful.

The articles selected for this book all focus on leveraging Java's capabilities for application development. The first challenge in developing a portable application is the user interface. The graphical user interfaces for different platforms all have different capabilities and deficiencies. The intuitive method for creating a universal class library for user interfaces is to provide the common subset of functionality shared by all existing user interfaces.

This approach is not adequate for most application developers, who need to provide drag-and-drop interfaces, flexible layouts, and other features users have come to expect and demand. Jeffrey Kay, Anil Hemrajani, and Cory Bear all describe strategies and techniques for developing user interfaces and satisfying these basic requirements using Java's Abstract Window Toolkit (AWT).

For Java to truly gain acceptance as an application language, programmers need to understand the nuances of the language, identify the differences between Java and the environments with which they are familiar, and ultimately migrate their existing codebase. Gary Aitken describes the differences between C++ and Java, and Andrew Wilson discusses migrating existing Windows applications to Java. Then there are situations when Java alone simply isn't good enough. Anil Hemrajani and Robi Khan describe how to call native C code from Java. Gary Aitken then explains how to generate documentation from Java source files.

Java was designed with the network in mind, so it's no surprise that it's well suited for multi-tier client/server environments. David Mitchell's war cry is "just enough Java," as he describes strategies for architecting and integrating Java in client/server applications. For simple two-tier applications, Andrew Wilson explains how to use JDBC to access databases. Cliff Berg tells us how to write CORBA applications in Java.

One of the biggest complaints about Java is its performance. Paul Tyma presents tips for improving Java performance, while Bruce Eckel tells us how to use garbage collection to achieve faster speeds.

Many professional programmers have experienced the frustration of designing and implementing good, technically-sound applications, and then never seeing the product go to market or gain acceptance. Java is unique because it has already won market acceptance. The future of Java lies in your hands. We hope you'll find these articles invaluable in harnessing the potential of Java.

Java User-Interface Design

Jeffrey Kay

IBM infoMarket is one of the first major web-based search services to imple-ment a user interface written entirely in Java. This Java interface accomplishes two things. First, it provides advanced capabilities similar to those available in stand-alone applications. Second, the software demonstrates Java's capabilities in a serious and significant application. Some of the most interesting Java software on the Internet is presented as more of a window decoration than a primary interface. This Java interface brings users functionality previously found only in software natively installed on the users' computers.

IBM infoMarket (http://www.infomarket.ibm.com/) lets users search multiple source databases simultaneously. These databases are categorized by subject area and name, providing a way to select which sources are searched. Users may perform simple searches by entering keywords or a more-advanced Boolean query. The search results in a "hit" list that returns the title of the content, an exhibit, date, author, relevance rank, and price.

The original IBM infoMarket interface uses HTML forms. The simple search screen includes an edit box for keywords and the source list coded as a series of check-box list elements. The search returns a hit list as an HTML page, 25 hits at a time. The original interface, including the generation of the

Jeffrey specializes in software design and development for IBM. He can be contacted at jeffrey_kay@vnet.ibm.com. Reprinted courtesy of Dr. Dobb's Sourcebook.

search screen, source list, hit list, and user-requested data reductions, is implemented almost entirely as CGI scripts.

While HTML and CGI comprise a viable approach, a more interactive interface enhances usability. The HTML version requires users to page forward and backward to refine a query because the search page and the results page are separate. And because the results are all page oriented, the hit list is limited to a quantity that is reasonably visible on a screen.

The design goals of the Java version were to improve the overall usability and to increase functionality. The hierarchical nature of the sources is easily represented by a hierarchical listbox with expanding and collapsing entries. This listbox allows users to see just topic areas or to delve deeper into the available sources for a particular topic area. Users can even mix and match topic areas and particular sources if it makes sense for a query.

Users can experiment with different ways of formulating queries by toggling between the simple search and advanced search. The search-entry fields retain the terms as users try different searches to see which results in the best hit list.

By displaying the results as a multicolumn listbox or grid control, users can access a wider range of functions, including sorting and selecting. In addition, a multicolumn listbox can hold many more lines than might make sense for HTML-based output.

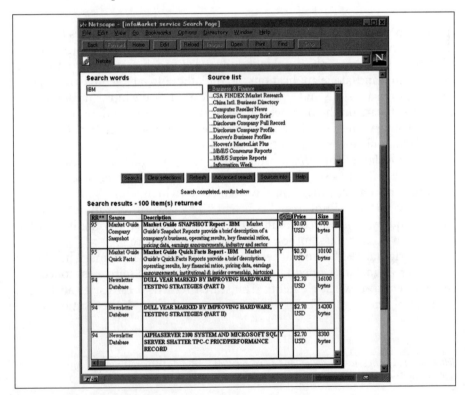

Figure 1: *IBM infoMarket service Java search screen.*

In the end, the user interface should adopt the style of most interactive applications, with the search query, source list, and results list residing on the same screen. Users then have all of the information in view when searching.

Figure 1 is the enhanced, Java-based IBM infoMarket user interface. The search-word entry portion of the window flips between the simple search and the advanced search. This source list appears to the right in an expanding and collapsing entry listbox. The results are in the bottom part of the panel in a single multicolumn listbox. In the center of the listbox are the buttons used to control the operations and a message label indicating the status of the operation.

Basic Applet Structure

The basic applet structure is a single flow from the entry of search terms to the review of results. The interface to the web server is implemented through CGI scripts. In early implementations, a CGI script parsed the HTML pages returned by our production system, but later versions of the software use CGI scripts that return "raw" output in a format easily parsed in the Java code. All CGI interfaces are implemented using the GET method to avoid the additional code necessary to implement a POST in Java.

The sources listbox is a derivation of the standard Java *ListBox* class. The listbox keeps track of which list elements are expandable and which are not. In addition, the titles of the sources are matched with the terms that are returned as part of the CGI call to the web server when executing a search.

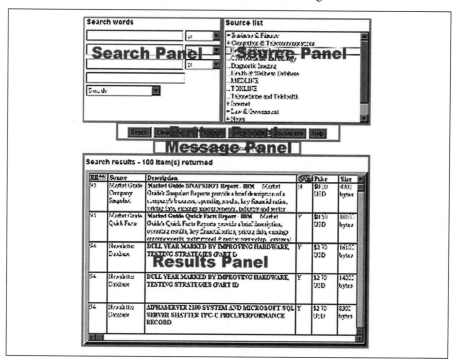

Figure 2: *Panels of the main display.*

The entire screen display is implemented using a series of panels. The outermost panel and all but two of the inner panels use the *GridBagLayout* Manager. Although it is the most complicated layout manager in the Java Abstract Windows Toolkit (AWT), the *GridBagLayout* Manager is also the most functional when the user interface requires precise layout instructions. It allows each component in the panel to be placed precisely with respect to its neighbors. The only panels that do not use the *GridBagLayout* are the Message panel (*BorderLayout*) and the Button panel (*FlowLayout*). Figure 2 shows each of the panels in the display.

To easily switch between the simple and advanced search options, each entry screen is built into a separate panel. When pressing the toggle button (designated "Simple search" or "Advanced search" depending on what is currently displayed), the applet quickly rebuilds the interface using the appropriate display panel. The rebuilding of the display is also aided by having each of the main interface components in its own panel, reducing the complexity of the code. Figure 3 is a subsection of the search screen with the advanced-search panel visible.

Threads

Threads play a minor role in the applet, implementing the "cancel search" functionality and the asynchronous collection of status information during a search. The use of threads allows the applet to perform some minor functions without polluting object encapsulations in the code.

The cancel search function uses a thread to allow the search operation to run independently. The applet can then continue processing messages in the message queue, a necessary function when user input is required. When a search starts (a user presses the "Search" button), the search thread starts and the Search button is retitled "Cancel search." All other buttons are disabled. If the Cancel search button is pressed, the search thread is stopped using a *Thread.stop()* function call.

The status functionality is implemented in a similar fashion. The search code is fully encapsulated in a single object, a derivation of the multicolumn listbox class. That class initiates the search CGI call, retrieves the results, and displays them. The search thread, while running, polls that object every half second to find out how many elements it currently has in the list. This method informs the user that something is happening while the search results are retrieved, and does not burden the Java applet significantly.

The Multicolumn Listbox

The most interesting class in the applet is the multicolumn listbox (*MCList*). While not the most ideal or efficient implementation of a basic grid control, the code employs many of the more subtle Java language elements. In particular, a C++ software developer may not be familiar with some of these techniques because they are unavailable in C++. It is also the one place in the code that extensive work had to be done to ensure compatibility across platforms.

The multicolumn listbox is implemented as the public class *MCList* (available electronically on the CD-ROM), which encapsulates three subcomponents: horizontal and vertical scroll bars (*MCScrollbar*) and *MCCanvas*, an extension of the *Canvas* class. In addition, two public interface classes allow a developer to implement "owner-drawing" and "owner-defined sorting" objects that can be used in a cell.

MCList

MCList is an extension of the *Panel* class that implements many of the "pass-through" function calls. Since most of the functionality of the class resides in *MCCanvas*, *MCList* must expose certain function calls to provide a single interface point. An alternate approach would have been to build most of the functionality into *MCList* directly, but the encapsulation of the drawing routines in the *MCCanvas* class reduces the complexity of the code and takes advantage of the layout capabilities in Java. The constructors in *MCList* set up the number of rows and columns that the listbox must initially display. While the number of rows is variable, there are no provisions in this implementation to add columns. The *validate()* and *setFont()* functions have been overridden to ensure that the horizontal scroll bar limits are set properly. The vertical scroll bar increments by row count rather than pixel count, so its limits are only updated when the row count changes.

MCScrollbar

Perhaps the most frustrating thing about Java is its relative infancy. *MCScrollbar* is a class designed to address just that issue. Because of the variations in Java implementations, the limits and line- and page-increment values of the default scroll bars were inconsistent. To work around these problems, the *MCScrollbar* class overrides several of the *Scrollbar* class functions and replaces them with equivalent functions that work better across platforms.

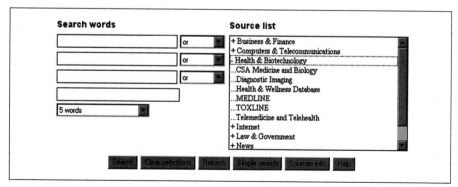

Figure 3: *Subsection of search screen showing advanced search panel.*

MCPaintable and MCSortable Interface Classes

Interface classes define functional interfaces that allow an object to provide functionality without having to define a new superclass. Specifically, the *MCSortable* and *MCPaintable* interface classes (Listings One and Two, respectively) allow an object stored in a cell to provide functions for painting and sorting itself even though the object's base class is *Object*. These classes are used to display the icon in the header row, to draw the description column with bold and plain fonts, and to sort columns alphabetically or numerically. The *MCImage* and *TitleAbstract* classes, private classes implemented as part of the main program, demonstrate the use of these classes (Listing Three).

The *MCImage* class defines an extension to the *Object* class that implements *MCPaintable* to draw a picture in a cell area. The *MCPaintable* class requires that the *paint()* function be implemented, which in this case just draws the image on the supplied *Graphics* object. Because the class is derived from the base *Object* class, it can be used as the contents of a cell.

The *TitleAbstract* class is more complicated, implementing both the *MCPaintable* and *MCSortable* interfaces. This is as close to multiple inheritance as Java permits. The *TitleAbstract* class extends *Object* (as required for use with *MCList*) and implements the *toString()* function to return an appropriate value. The *paint()* function draws the title string in bold while the abstract part is drawn using a plain text face. The *lessthan()* and *greaterthan()* functions compare the joined title and abstract to the string value of any other object.

MCCanvas

MCCanvas is the centerpiece of the multicolumn listbox. It draws the rows and maintains the values of the cells. Each cell value must be derived from the *Object* class and all values are stored in *Vector*s, one per column. The column headers are also stored in a single *Vector* and one additional *Vector* is defined to store the sort index. Because the widths of the columns are fixed, a single array of integers is defined to hold the width of each column. The width of a column is defined in characters based on the average width of the characters in the selected font.

As rows are added, cell values are set to zero-length *String*s. The cell values are set individually using the *setValue()* function, where the arguments are the row, the column, and the *Object* to be stored in the cell. As cells are set, they are painted using the *paintCell()* function. This function is called directly, rather than using a *repaint()* call, to update the display synchronously.

The *paint()* function itself is split into several function calls so that individual parts of the display can be drawn as needed or as part of a global update. The *paint()* function calls the drawing routines for all of the display components:

- *paintHeaders()* paints the header row of the listbox.
- *paintRow()* paints a single row of the display.
- *paintCell()* paints a single cell.

The *paintHeaders()* function does not call *paintCell()* even though *paintCell()* duplicates much of *paintHeaders()*'s functionality. The *paintHeaders()* function does some additional manipulation of the cell contents before it is displayed (it adds "**" to the primary sort-column header), preventing the use of *paintCell()* in its present form.

The *paintCell()* function draws the contents of each cell. Because of the possibility of a cell implementing its own painting routine, *paintCell()* must check the object before it is drawn to see if it implements the *MCPaintable* interface class. It does this using the *instanceof* operator, an operator that can test the object to see what classes it instantiates. If the object is an instance of the *MCPaintable* class, it is recast and its *paint()* function is called. If the object is just a string, it is automatically fit into the cell area using word wrapping. Figure 4, an excerpt from *paintCell()*, shows this code.

The *paintCell()* function uses the *create()* method of the *Graphics* class to create subsections for drawing. This is required because only one clipping rectangle can be established for a *Graphics* object. When *paintCell()* is called, a new *Graphics* object is created based on the original *Graphics* object. This new *Graphics* object clips to the dimensions of the cell and is used for all subsequent graphics operations.

Sorting is implemented in *MCCanvas* using a low-tech insertion sort. Though there are many container classes provided with Java, no sorting functions are provided. The *sort()* function is called explicitly by the owner of the *MCList* object. During a sort, each object is tested with *instanceof* to see if it implements *MCSortable*; if it does, the *lessthan()* and *greaterthan()* functions of *MCSortable* are used for comparisons. If not, the object is sorted based on the value of the *toString()* function.

Lessons Learned

I encountered several problems using Java as a development language and environment. The good news, however, is that these are not inherent problems; almost all stem from Java's relative immaturity. As Java matures, many of these problems should go away.

The development platform was the Java Development Kit (JDK) Version 1.02 under Windows 95 with Netscape Navigator as the target platform. I wrote all of the code by hand using an editor and a make program, and used the JDK Appletviewer for development testing. When it became apparent that Navigator and the JDK Appletviewer did not function exactly the same, I was forced to use Navigator more extensively and earlier in the process than I desired. In most cases, the Appletviewer did a better job displaying the applet than Netscape Navigator.

Netscape Navigator 2.02 showed symptoms of memory problems. When the multicolumn listbox reached 100 elements, Netscape Navigator crashed. As a result, I reset my sights for Navigator 3.0 and beyond.

The *showDocument()* function is the Java function that retrieves documents in the search-results list. Because of a bug in early betas of Navigator 3, any document retrieved that was processed by a helper application crashed the browser. I developed a kludge using JavaScript. Instead of using the *showDocument()* function directly, *showDocument()* calls a JavaScript function and passes the document URL to that function. This changed the call from

showDocument("http:// xxx.xxx.xxx.xxx/ xxx.xxx");

to

showDocument("javascript:showdoc(\"http:// xxx.xxx.xxx.xxx/xxx.xxx\"));.

Of course, this prevented other browsers from retrieving documents, since only Navigator currently implements JavaScript. Navigator 3.0 beta 5 cured this problem.

Scroll bars continue to be a source of frustration. Each platform seems to have a different idea about the scroll-bar limits and page- and line-increment values. Some betas of Navigator had a bug that would not allow the page- and line-increment values to be changed from their defaults of 10 and 1, respectively. I coded *MCScrollbar* to eliminate this inconsistency by trapping most of the scroll-bar value sets.

Double clicking on a *Canvas* also proved troublesome. The *handleEvent()* function in *MCList* has several workarounds to address this problem. This problem initially manifested itself on UNIX/X-Windows and Macintosh platforms, where the double click could not be trapped, but even Navigator 3.0 beta 5 for Windows 95 exhibited this problem. The initial workaround counted Event.MOUSE_DOWN events, but this also proved inconsistent. A second workaround counted Event.MOUSE_UP events and this worked better. There are still double-click problems on some platforms.

A strange problem with the *setFont()* function occurred while building the *paint()* routine for the *TitleAbstract* class. Apparently, doing a *setFont()* while clicking on a scroll bar could cause a thread (or the main thread) to freeze. I attempted to correct the problem by disabling the multicolumn listbox during screen painting. This worked in most cases. Fortunately, it appears that this problem has vanished from later betas of Navigator 3.0.

Font problems across platforms also seem to exist. Java uses the "a-point-a-pixel" model: One point equals one pixel. On some Navigator implementations, the font metrics returned from a selected font were occasionally incorrect, sometimes even twice that of the selected font. The text on the screen looked okay and demonstrated that the system was returning the cor-

```
if (values[col].elementAt(realRow(row)) instanceof MCPaintable) {
    MCPaintable x = (MCPaintable)values[col].elementAt(realRow(row));
    x.paint(newg,this,widths[col]*aveWidth+Inset,Inset);
}
```

Figure 4: *Code excerpt from* paintCell() *showing the use of* instanceof.

rect font size, but the font metrics that the Java Virtual Machine returned were wrong. I found no particular workaround that was acceptable.

On Navigator 3.0 beta 5, invalidating the windows did not always result in a *repaint()* call. I corrected this by adding a *repaint()* call after the *invalidate()*. In addition, to prevent flickering on screen updates, the *update()* function of a component is overridden to just call *paint()*. This prevents the *update()* function from clearing the component area.

Conclusion

The IBM infoMarket Java user interface demonstrates great potential as a primary user interface. It improves usability and increases functionality. As the Java environment matures, this user interface and others like it will drive the World Wide Web into the universe of interactive applications.

Listing One

```
import java.awt.*;
import java.awt.image.*;
import java.applet.*;
import java.net.*;
import java.util.*;
import java.io.*;

// Code is provided "AS IS" for example purposes only, without warranty

public interface MCPaintable {
    abstract void paint(Graphics g, Object o,int width, int inset);
}
```

Listing Two

```
import java.awt.*;
import java.awt.image.*;
import java.applet.*;
import java.net.*;
import java.util.*;
import java.io.*;

// Code provided "AS IS" for example purposes only, without warranty
public interface MCSortable {
    abstract boolean lessthan(Object o);
    abstract boolean greaterthan(Object o);
}
```

Listing Three

```
import java.awt.*;
import java.awt.image.*;
import java.applet.*;
```

```
import java.net.*;
import java.util.*;
import java.io.*;

// Code provided "AS IS" for example purposes only, without warranty

class MCImage extends Object implements MCPaintable {
    Image image;
    public MCImage(Image i) {
        image = i;
    }
    public void paint(Graphics g, Object o,int width,int inset) {
        if (g == null) return;
        if (o instanceof ImageObserver) {
            g.drawImage(image,inset,0,(ImageObserver)o);
        }
    }
    public String toString() {
        return "Cryptolope";
    }
}
class TitleAbstract extends Object implements MCPaintable, MCSortable {
    String Title = "";
    String Abstract = "";

    public TitleAbstract(String t, String a) {
        Title = t;
        Abstract = a;
    }
    public String toString() {
        return Title + " " + Abstract;
    }
    public boolean lessthan(Object o) {
        return toString().compareTo(o.toString()) < 0;
    }
    public boolean greaterthan(Object o) {
        return toString().compareTo(o.toString()) > 0;
    }
    // void wrapString(Graphics g,String s,int w)

    public void paint(Graphics g, Object o,int width, int inset) {
        if (g == null) return;
        width -= inset;
        if (width <= 0) return; // hidden row
        String temp = "";
        FontMetrics fm = null;
        Font f = g.getFont();

        int col = 0;  // x coordinate
        int y = 0;  // y coordinate
        int lineheight = 0; // lineheight

        Font newFont = new Font(f.getName(),Font.BOLD,f.getSize());

        for(int i=0;i<2;i++) {
            StringTokenizer st = null;
            if (i == 0) {
                g.setFont(newFont);
                st = new StringTokenizer(Title);
```

```
                fm = g.getFontMetrics();
                y = fm.getMaxAscent();
            }
            else {
                g.setFont(f);
                fm = g.getFontMetrics();
                st = new StringTokenizer(Abstract);
            }
            lineheight = fm.getMaxAscent() + fm.getMaxDescent();
            while (st.hasMoreTokens()) {
                String tok = st.nextToken();
                if (temp == "") {
                    temp = tok;
                }
                else {
                    if (fm.stringWidth(temp + " " + tok) < width - col) {
                        temp += " " + tok;
                    }
                    else {
                        if ((col + fm.stringWidth(temp) > width) && (col != 0)) {
                            col = 0;
                            y += lineheight;
                            if (fm.stringWidth(temp + " " + tok) < width - col) {
                                g.drawString(temp,col,y);
                                col = 0;
                                y += lineheight;
                                temp = tok;
                            }
                        }
                        else {
                            g.drawString(temp,col+inset,y);
                            col = 0;
                            y += lineheight;
                            temp = tok;
                        }
                    }
                }
            }
            if (temp != "") {
                g.drawString(temp,col+inset,y);
                col += fm.stringWidth(temp)+fm.stringWidth("XX");
                temp = "";
                if (col > width) {
                    col = 0;
                    y += lineheight;
                }
            }
        }                    \
    }
}
```

End Listings

The Java Abstract Window Toolkit

Anil Hemrajani

One of the most important packages (class libraries) provided in the Java API is the Abstract Window Toolkit (AWT). AWT includes a complete set of classes for developing portable GUI applications in Java. It provides classes for basic GUI controls, containers, event handling, component placement, fonts, colors, drawing, images, sounds, and more. The main benefits of AWT over other GUI class libraries is that Java applications can run on all supported platforms (without recompiling or relinking), and Java applets can be accessed from anywhere by connecting to the Internet via a Java-compatible browser.

Java programs can be written as applications, applets, or both. Each is created by compiling Java source code into bytecodes using the Java compiler (javac). Figure 1 shows a sample text-editor application on Windows 95, and Figure 2 shows an applet version, also on Windows 95. Both are generated by the same Java program—TextEdit.java (available electronically on the CD-ROM).

Applets are invoked by a Java-compatible Web browser or the appletviewer utility (available with the Java Development Kit). Both require an HTML file with an <APPLET> tag that points to a Java class file. This file must contain a class that subclasses from the *Applet* class. The *Applet* class contains the methods

Anil currently provides software engineering and training consulting services to a Fortune 500 corporation in McLean, VA. He can be contacted at anil@patriot.net or via http://www.patriot.net/users/anil/. Reprinted courtesy of Dr. Dobb's Journal.

```
cs = new Choice();
cbb = new Checkbox("Bold");
buttonPanel = new Panel();
buttonPanel.add(new Button(MI_NEW));
ta = new TextArea(30, 80);
Menu fm  = new Menu("File");
fm.add(new MenuItem(TextEdit.MI_SAVE));
tURL = new TextField(80);
```

Example 1: *Creating GUI Components with default settings.*

init(), *start()*, *stop()*, and *destroy()*, which are invoked when an applet is initialized, started, stopped, and destroyed, respectively. These methods can be overridden by the subclass.

Java applications are invoked via the Java interpreter by providing it the name of a class. The interpreter searches for the class file (classname.*class*) in the directories indicated in the CLASSPATH environment variable or the current directory if CLASSPATH has not been set. The name of the class in this file must match the name passed to the interpreter. Additionally, it must contain a *main()* method with the signature *public static void main(String args[])*.

The basic steps for developing a Java application or applet include:

- Creating GUI components.

- Adding them in containers.

- Using layout managers to position components in the containers (optional).

- Handling events generated by user input.

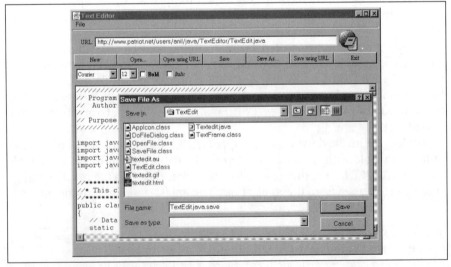

Figure 1: *Text-editor application on Windows 95.*

```
(a)   fontPanel.setLayout(new FlowLayout(FlowLayout.LEFT));

(b)   buttonPanel.setLayout(new GridLayout(1, 7));

(c)   setLayout(new BorderLayout(1, 2));
      add("North",  topPanel);
      add("Center", ta);
      add("South",  statusBar);
```

Example 2: *(a) Using* FlowLayout *to place controls from left to right with left justification; (b)* GridLayout *automatically resizes all buttons to equal sizes; (c) using* BorderLayout *to place components.*

Basic GUI Components

The GUI components Java currently supports include Buttons, Canvases, Radio Buttons, Checkboxes, Choices, Dialogs, FileDialogs, Frames, Labels, Lists, Menus, Panels, ScrollBars, TextAreas, and TextFields. TextEdit.java (which generated Figures 1 and 2) uses most of these components. Components are created by using the *new* keyword. Most components can be created with default settings by passing in values; see Example 1 (excerpted from TextEdit.java).

All GUI components inherit from the *Component* class, which provides several methods for operations on components. These include checking the bounds of a component, getting/setting a component's font, enabling/disabling the component, getting/setting colors, requesting/moving focus, hiding/show-

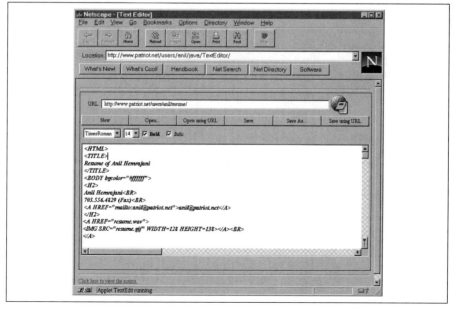

Figure 2: *Text-editor applet on Windows 95.*

ing the component, resizing the component, moving the component, and more.

Containers

AWT Containers are GUI objects that group components in a specified area of a window. AWT provides two major types of containers—Windows and Panels—that are implemented by the *Window* and *Panel* classes, respectively. Both classes are subclasses of the *Container* class, which inherits from the *Component* class. Additional container classes include *Frame*, *Dialog*, and *Applet*. *Frame* and *Dialog* subclass from the *Window* class, whereas the *Applet* class subclasses from the *Panel* class.

Containers used in TextEdit.java include a Frame and a Panel. Figure 3 illustrates how this application uses these containers. Notice how panels can not only contain other components, but also other panels. For instance, *topPanel.add("North", urlPanel);* (extracted from TextEdit.java) adds a panel (containing choice lists and checkboxes) inside another panel. The line *add("North", topPanel);* adds another *Panel* object to the applet, which itself is a subclass of *Panel*.

Since applets cannot serve as an application's main *Frame* window, they require a browser or Java application to provide this frame window for them. TextEdit.java creates a frame window when it is run as an application, then creates an instance of the *TextEdit* class (a subclass of the *Applet* class) and calls its *init()* method (*te.init()*) just as a browser would.

Layout Managers

Layout Managers arrange components inside containers and automatically reposition (and sometimes resize) them every time the container changes its appearance. This simplifies the task of figuring out absolute coordinates for components. Additionally, this ensures that the components will have the best possible appearance in browsers and different monitor resolutions.

AWT currently provides five predefined Layout Managers:

- *FlowLayout*, which places components in a simple left-to-right order.

- *GridLayout*, which places components in rows and columns after resizing all of them to the same size.

- *BorderLayout*, which places the components in five areas: north, south, east, west, and center.

- *CardLayout*, which is useful if an area in a window can contain different components at different times based on the state of the application.

- *GridBagLayout*, which allows components to be placed vertically and horizontally without requiring them to be the same size.

The alternatives to using the predefined layout managers include designing a custom layout manager (See "Your Own Java Layout Manager," by Cory Bear, later in this book, and "How Do I Create a Layout Manager," by Cliff Berg, *Dr. Dobb's Journal*, September, 1996) or doing without them using absolute positioning. Custom layout managers can be created by providing an implementation for the *LayoutManager* interface (abstract class). Absolute positioning of components is not recommended, especially for applets that can be viewed through different browsers.

TextEdit.java uses *BorderLayout*, *FlowLayout*, *GridLayout*, and *GridBagLayout* to lay out its various panels (see Figure 3). For example, the panel containing the font controls uses *FlowLayout* to place its controls from left to right with left justification; see Example 2(a). The panel containing the push buttons uses the *GridLayout* with settings of one row and seven columns (corresponding to the seven buttons). *GridLayout* automatically resizes all buttons in this panel to equal sizes; see Example 2(b). The applet panel uses a *BorderLayout* to place its components in three of the five areas available with this layout; see Example 2(c).

Event Handling

Once an application's screen has been designed, you make it operational by reacting to events generated by user input. All events are handled in a component's subclass by overriding the *handleEvent* method. Alternatively, event-specific methods can be implemented in the subclass such as *action, keyDown, mouseEnter, mouseExit, mouseMove, mouseUp, mouseDown,* and *mouseDrag.*

Events in AWT are passed up in a component's hierarchy; in other words, a subclass gets a crack at the event before its parent class does. If the event is handled by a class, it should return a value of *true* to indicate that the event has been handled, or *false* if the event was not handled. A component's subclass can also invoke its parent event-handler method directly (*return super.handleEvent(evt);*).

The *TextEdit* class in TextEdit.java uses *handleEvent* to react to all events generated by controls inside the applet panel; see Example 3(a). Additionally, *TextEdit* handles all events generated by the *TextFrame* class. Since *TextFrame* is designed primarily to provide a frame for the applet, it forwards all its events to the *handleEvent* method in *TextEdit*; see Example 3(b).

More on the Java UI API

Java also provides an API for working with fonts, colors, drawing, images, sounds, and text-based user interfaces. The *Font* class can be used for setting the font of a GUI component: Create an instance of the *Font* class with the font name, style (bold, italic, normal), and size, then use the component's *setFont()* method; see Example 4(a).

The *Color* class provides some predefined static colors (*black, blue, cyan, darkGray, gray, green, lightGray, magenta, orange, pink, red, white,* and *yellow*)

```
(a)    public boolean handleEvent(Event evt)
       {
           if (evt.id == Event.WINDOW_DESTROY)
                terminate(0);
           else
           if (evt.id == Event.ACTION_EVENT)
           ...

(b)    if (te != null)
           return te.handleEvent(evt);
```

Example 3: *(a) Using* handleEvent *to react to events generated by the controls;*
(b) forwarding events to the handleEvent *method.*

```
(a)    cbb.setFont(new Font(cbb.getFont().getName(),
                Font.BOLD, cbb.getFont().getSize()));

(b)    ta.setBackground(Color.blue);
       g.setColor(getBackground());

(c)    g.f ill3DRect(0, 0, size().width, 2, false);

(d)    play(getCodeBase(), "hello.au");
```

Example 4: *(a) Using the* setFont() *method; (b) using* setColor *method;*
(c) generating a 3-D look; (d) using an .au audio file.

for setting the background or foreground of a component. Additional colors
can be generated using RGB (0-255) or HSB (0.0-1.0) values. To set the back-
ground/foreground of a component, use the *setBackground/setForeground*
methods provided in the *Component* class. To set the default color for a drawing object, use that object's *setColor* method, as in Example 4(b).

AWT provides classes and methods for drawing lines, oval shapes, poly-
gons, rectangles, and rounded rectangles. Additionally, some of these drawing
objects can have a 3-D look, a highlighted look, or both; see Example 4(c).

Java currently provides a limited API for multimedia processing. Methods
are provided for reading, displaying, and manipulating images in GIF and
JPEG formats. Also, simple animation can be performed by displaying multiple image files or drawing objects in the same or different areas of a window.
This technique is analogous to playing several frames from a reel of film to
produce a picture in motion. Java also provides sound support in applets via
methods such as *play()*. As of this article, only Sun's .au audio files (8-bit μ-
law, 8000Hz, one channel) are supported; see Example 4(d).

Text-based user interfaces generally involve the use of standard-output, standard-error, and standard-input devices. Java provides access to these devices via static variables in its *System* class (*System.out*, *System.err*, and *System.in*). For example, a sample message can be displayed to the standard-output device with *System.out.println("Hello world!");*.

Compiling and Running TextEdit.java

You can compile TextEdit.java from the command line by entering *javac Text-Edit.java*. Once a Java bytecode file (.class file) has been created, it can be copied to any supported platform and accessed without having to recompile or relink. To run a Java application (such as TextEdit.java), type *java TextEdit*. To run the applet version, put the HTML code *<applet code=TextEdit.class width=600 height=400></applet>* in a file (sample.html, for example) and pull it up in a Java-compatible browser, or use the appletviewer utility.

Future of Java

Java's future is promising. It is robust, object-oriented, and portable (source and bytecode). Java comes bundled with a suite of classes for GUI, multi-threading, networking, file I/O, and the like. To add to this, APIs for database access (Java Database Connectivity), more robust multimedia processing, and remote object access are in the works. Finally, several powerful Java IDEs are already on the market.

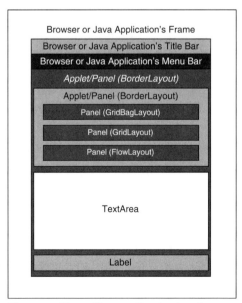

Figure 3: *Text-editor application/applet.*

Your Own Java Layout Manager

Cory Bear

While a small Java applet creates excitement with eye-catching animation or scrolling text, Java can be used for purposes more sophisticated than decorating your Web page. For example, larger applets with display components such as buttons, text fields, tables, and so on can be used as powerful, interactive user interfaces. The challenge in designing a large Java applet with many display components is finding a way to lay out those components attractively. How do you make text fields line up, or put a button in the correct spot? Java developers find the tools in the Abstract Window Toolkit (AWT) a big help, but many quickly learn that they need to design their own Java layout manager for advanced layout requirements.

This article explains how I designed a layout manager called *StackLayout* and provides useful tips on designing your own layout manager. *StackLayout*,

Cory is a software engineer with an interest in Java, Web page development, and VRML. Reprinted courtesy of Web Techniques.

21

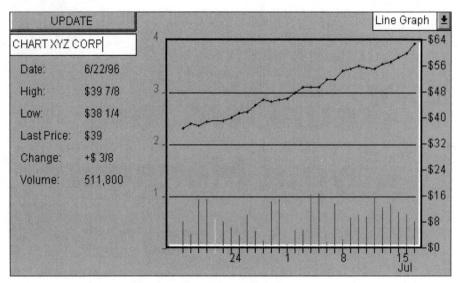

Figure 1: *Interface created using a Java layout manager.*

shown in Listing One, stacks display components one on top of another, so they all have the same width but different heights. For example, it is used in the applet shown in Figure 1 to lay out the "update" button, the "chart XYZ corp" text field, and a table of stock-quote information.

Java Layout Managers

Java provides five layout managers in the Abstract Window Toolkit (AWT), a package in the standard Java library: *BorderLayout*; *CardLayout*; *FlowLayout*; *GridLayout*; and *GridBagLayout*.

BorderLayout divides a window into five areas: north, south, east, west, and center. Each area holds one display component, placed on the window in a position corresponding to its area name. For example, the north component is placed on the top of the window, south is placed on the bottom of the window, and so on. *BorderLayout* is most useful for simple dialog boxes and windows that hold fewer than five display components.

CardLayout makes a window act like a Rolodex. It has a drop-down menu that allows the user to view a menu of "card" names and choose which card to display. Only one card may be displayed at a time—the others are hidden until the user chooses a different card.

FlowLayout, the default layout option for Java applets, is modeled after a type-writer. It lays out display components in a row from the left edge of a window to the right. When it reaches the right edge of the window, it starts a new row. *FlowLayout* works best when there are a small number of display components.

```
public class myApplet extends java.applet.Applet {
    public void init() {
        add("north", new java.awt.Button());
        add("south", new java.awt.TextField());
        add("columbia", new java.awt.Label());
    }
}
```

Example 1: *Creating a new applet.*

```
public class myApplet extends java.applet.Applet {
    public void init() {
        setLayout(new java.awt.BorderLayout());
        ...
    }
}
```

Example 2: *Specifying* BorderLayout *as the layout manager.*

GridLayout lays out display components on the squares of an imaginary checkerboard. First, it divides the window into a grid of identically sized squares, and then puts each display component into its own square, resizing the component as necessary until it fits the square. This layout option is most useful if all of the display components look attractive with exactly the same widths and heights. *GridLayout* also allows a grid of identically sized rectangles if you prefer that to squares.

GridBagLayout is an advanced version of *GridLayout* that allows display components to span more than one square. *GridBagLayout* is the most powerful layout manager in the AWT, and arguably the most difficult to use.

In Practice

The source code for a typical Java applet begins by defining a subclass of the *Applet* class, like *myApplet*, shown in Example 1. A subclass of the *Applet* class is an empty container, to which you add display components using the *add()* method. The button, text field, and label components in Example 1 are added to *myApplet* by this method and assigned arbitrary names ("north," "south," and "columbia").

The *add()* method does not control how components are arranged on the screen, so you must call the *setLayout()* method to specify a layout manager to do that. In Example 2, *setLayout()* specifies that *BorderLayout* is a layout manager that will be used to arrange components in *myApplet*. If you do not specify a layout manager using the *setLayout()* method, *FlowLayout* will be used by default.

Rolling Your Own

If none of the aforementioned layout options meets your needs, you must write your own Java layout manager. Java developers often have custom layout needs, because many kinds of layouts are impossible with the five AWT layout options. For example, I was unable to stack components one on top of the other so that all of the components had the same width but different heights. I tried to use *GridLayout*, but it forced all of the display components to have the same height. This meant that the table of quote information shrunk, and the button and text field expanded, as shown in Figure 2.

A Java layout manager implements the *LayoutManager* interface using five required methods: *preferredLayoutSize()*; *minimumLayoutSize()*; *layoutContainer()*; *addLayoutComponent()*; and *removeLayoutComponent()*.

Java calls these methods when a container is resized, or whenever it needs to arrange components within a container. The first method Java calls is usually *preferredLayoutSize()*, because that's how Java finds out how big the container should be. The preferred layout size is the length and the width of a rectangular area on the screen large enough to comfortably display the components.

The *preferredLayoutSize()* method in the *StackLayout* class computes the cumulative height of all the display components, and the width of the widest display component. It also takes into account the "vertical gap" between display components and the insets, or margins, surrounding them; see Figure 3.

Some layout managers also use the *minimumLayoutSize()* method to tell Java the length and the width of a rectangular area large enough to accommodate the display components so that they are squished, but still usable. *StackLayout* doesn't have this feature—it defines the minimum layout size to be the same as the preferred layout size, as shown in Figure 4.

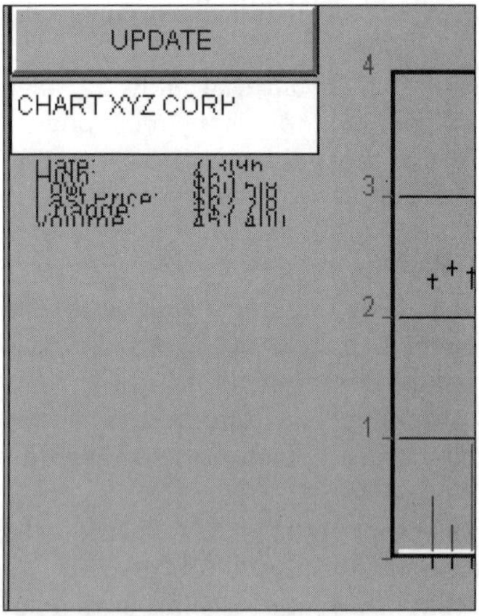

Once Java knows how much screen real estate is required by a container, it calls the *layoutContainer()* method to arrange the display components within the container. The *layoutContainer()* method must call the *reshape()* method of each component in the container in order to set that component's (x, y) coordinates and size. In Java, components know the preferred size, but will not assume that size by default: If the

Figure 2: GridLayout *forces all display components to have exactly the same height.*

```
public java.awt.Dimension preferredLayoutSize(java.awt.Container parent)
        {
    java.awt.Insets      insets = parent.insets();
    int                  ncomponents = parent.countComponents();
    int                  w = 0;
    int                  h = 0;

        for (int i = 0 ; i < ncomponents ; i++) {
            java.awt.Component comp = parent.getComponent(i);
            java.awt.Dimension d = comp.preferredSize();
            if (w < d.width) {
                w = d.width;
            }
            h += d.height;
            if (i != 0) {
                h += this.vgap;
            }
        }
        return new java.awt.Dimension(insets.left + insets.right + w,
            insets.top + insets.bottom + h);
    }
```

Figure 3: *Code for the* preferredLayoutSize() *method in* StackLayout.

layout manager fails to call the *reshape()* method for a component, then that component will not be displayed.

In the case of the *StackLayout* class, the *layoutContainer()* method stacks the display components so that all the components have the same width but different heights. It starts positioning the components at the top of the container and moves toward the bottom, widening each to the width of the container. The top of the container is the (x, y) coordinate at the top, left-hand side of the container. This coordinate is usually (0, 0), but if the container has an inset, then the top may be offset slightly. *StackLayout* also needs to know the width of the widest display component, because all of the other display components will be widened to match it. The width is obtained from the *preferredLayoutSize()* method; see Figure 5.

A layout-manager class must have at least two other methods: *addLayoutComponent()* and *removeLayoutComponent()*. These methods tell the layout manager the names of various display components. Once a layout manager has been created, the only way a developer can give it guidance about sizing or positioning a component is by a component's name. For example, *BorderLayout* treats components named north, south, east, and west specially, in that it positions them according to their names. However, most layout managers, including *StackLayout*, do not care what components are named. In these layout managers, the *addLayoutComponent()* and *removeLayoutComponent()* methods are stubs without any functionality. Technically, these methods must be

```
public java.awt.Dimension minimumLayoutSize(java.awt.Container parent) {
    return preferredLayoutSize(parent);
}
```

Figure 4: *Code for the* minimumLayoutSize() *method.*

```
public void layoutContainer(java.awt.Container parent) {
    java.awt.Insets insets = parent.insets();
    int x = insets.left;
    int y = insets.top;
    int w = this.preferredLayoutSize(parent).width;
    int ncomponents = parent.countComponents();
    for (int i = 0; i < ncomponents; ++i) {
        java.awt.Component comp = parent.getComponent(i);
        java.awt.Dimension d = comp.preferredSize();
        comp.reshape(x, y, w, d.height);
        y += (d.height + this.vgap);
    }
}
```

Figure 5: *The* layoutContainer() *method.*

```
class StackLayout implements java.awt.LayoutManager {
        int vgap;
        public StackLayout(int vgap) {
                this.vgap = vgap;
        }
        ...
```

Figure 6: *Passing the vertical gap spacing as a parameter.*

present in order to implement the *LayoutManager* interface, but they do not actually do anything.

A layout manager usually has a *public* constructor that's called when an instance of the layout manager is created, a convenient time to specify additional layout parameters. For example, the constructor for the *StackLayout* class takes the vertical gap spacing between components as a parameter; see Figure 6.

Once completed, a new layout manager is installed with a container's *add()* method. The new layout manager will then control arrangement of display components on the screen.

End Note

You can see the *StackLayout* in action by pointing your browser to http://www.softbear.com/java/mktview, where you'll find MKTVIEW, a freeware Java applet that allows you to chart stock prices and volume over time. You can view the current quote, including the ticker symbol, last price, price change, high price, low price, and volume. In addition, a daily chart displays recent market history. The source code for the stock-charting applet is also available from this page.

Listing One

```
/**
 * A layoutManager which stacks components one on top of the other,
 * regardless of their size.
 */

class StackLayout implements java.awt.LayoutManager {

 int vgap;

 public StackLayout(int vgap) {
  this.vgap = vgap;
 }

 public void addLayoutComponent(java.lang.String name, java.awt.Component
comp) {}

 public java.awt.Dimension preferredLayoutSize(java.awt.Container parent)
  java.awt.Insets insets = parent.insets();
  int  ncomponents = parent.countComponents();
  int  w = 0;
  int  h = 0;

  for (int i = 0 ; i < ncomponents ; i++) {
   java.awt.Component comp = parent.getComponent(i);
   java.awt.Dimension d = comp.preferredSize();
   if (w < d.width) {
    w = d.width;
   }
   h += d.height;
   if (i != 0) {
    h += this.vgap;
   }
  }
  return new java.awt.Dimension(insets.left + insets.right + w,
   insets.top + insets.bottom + h);
 }

 public void layoutContainer(java.awt.Container parent) {
  java.awt.Insets insets = parent.insets();
  int x = insets.left;
  int y = insets.top;
  int w = this.preferredLayoutSize(parent).width;
```

```
 int ncomponents = parent.countComponents();
 for (int i = 0; i < ncomponents; ++i) {
  java.awt.Component comp = parent.getComponent(i);
  java.awt.Dimension d = comp.preferredSize();
  comp.reshape(x, y, w, d.height);
  y += (d.height + this.vgap);
 }
}

public java.awt.Dimension minimumLayoutSize(java.awt.Container parent) {
 return preferredLayoutSize(parent);
}

public void removeLayoutComponent(java.awt.Component comp) {}
}
```

End Listings

Moving from C++ to Java

Gary Aitken

If you haven't been banished to a desert island, then you've heard about Java and its potential impact on both developers and users. In this article, I'll highlight some of the differences between Java and C++. My purpose is not to teach you how to program in Java, but rather to make you aware of potential problems and opportunities when moving from C++ to Java. I'll provide brief explanations of those concepts with which you may not be familiar, although I won't provide in-depth coverage of how they work or how to use them. Keep in mind that these are the major differences as I perceive them and are the result of my personal experiences with Java.

Java Executes on a Virtual Machine

Java source is not compiled into normal machine code. It is translated into code for a virtual machine specifically designed to support Java's features. A Java interpreter then executes the translated code. No link step is required; the interpreter dynamically links in additional classes on demand; see Figure 1.

Gary has been the technical lead and chief architect for a large, commercial, UNIX-based C++ toolkit for the past seven years. Reprinted courtesy of Dr. Dobb's Journal.

Java is Totally Object Oriented

Java is a totally object-oriented language. This means *everything* you do must be done via a method invocation (member function call) for a Java object. To start with, there is no such thing as a stand-alone *main* function. Instead, you must begin to view your whole application as an object; an object of a particular class. But what class? Most Java applications simply make a new class derived from the primitive Java *Object* class and implement everything they need, but you can save much time and improve consistency between applications by creating a base application class to handle features common to all applications.

The strict, object-oriented nature of the Java environment means existing C and C++ code can't be used directly; the same goes for system calls. In C++, you can get to existing C procedures, including most system calls, simply by declaring the C procedure as outside of the normal C++ namespace using the *extern "C"* syntax.

In Java, there's a similar escape hatch, but it isn't nearly as simple to use. You must define a native method, whose purpose is to interface to the C function, then provide the glue to connect to it. The Java environment provides tools to help with this task, but the whole process certainly isn't as trivial as the C++ *extern* escape. Interfacing to C++ classes is even more complex, involving the interface to C classes and the normal problems of invoking C++ functions and member functions from C. Fortunately, many of the more-common system-utility functions are already provided via methods in the *System* class, but

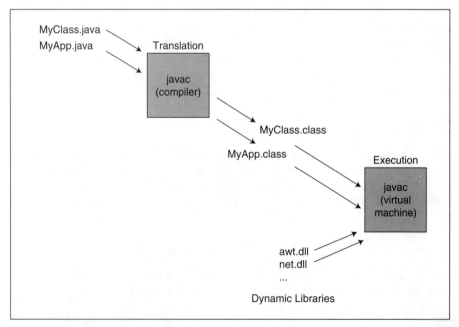

Figure 1: *The Java development environment.*

these obviously won't include any of the useful procedures or classes you may have built up over the years. Save delving into this until you really need to.

Separate Header Files don't Exist in Java

In Java, everything about a class is contained in a single file. The signature of a method appears in only one place, and the implementation of a method must appear simultaneously with its declaration. The advantage of this is that it is more difficult to mistakenly program using files that are out of synchronization with the implementation, or to get a library that is missing the implementation of some member function. Class declarations (function signatures and public variables) are available to the Java translator even from the binary output of a compilation, so no additional header files are needed, just the compiled object file.

The disadvantages of this are primarily related to how we program. Many C++ programmers use header files more or less as documentation. To see what the interface to a particular member function is, you bring up the header file and find the function. You can usually look at most header files on a single page and get a good idea of how a particular class should be used. In Java, there is no such concise summary available. Since the code to implement a method must appear with the method definition, and the code for a single function frequently occupies a page or more, it is difficult to look at any Java source and get an impression of how the class should be used. You must have adequate documentation for any classes you intend to use, which should go without saying, but often documentation is sorely lacking when you are dealing with in-house-designed classes or classes that are not part of a fully supported commercial product.

Two tools supplied in current Java environments which should help with this are javap, a disassembler that prints class signatures, and javadoc, which produces HTML documentation from comments embedded in source files.

Packages Partition the Namespace in Java

One problem large C++ projects encounter is namespace pollution—how can you ensure that some other developer working on a different aspect of a project won't create a class with the same name as a totally different class in another part of the project? Worse yet, a vendor may deliver a library with a class that uses a name that you have already used. There are various ways to minimize these problems in C++, but a project may be well underway before the problem rears its ugly head, and correcting it then is painful and costly.

Java addresses this problem using a concept called "Packages," which effectively partitions the name space for classes by collecting classes into named packages. Two classes with the same name, in different packages, are still unique. The key, then, is to be sure related classes are collected into their own package.

Remember, however, that Java does not solve the general problem of name collision. Extending a base class and thereby causing a collision with a derived class will remain a problem. For example, if your favorite vendor has supplied a set of classes that you use as base classes and your derived class has a method named *foo*, you will have problems if the next version of the vendor's class contains a new method also named *foo*.

Exceptions are First-Class Characteristics in Java

In C++, exceptions and exception handling are rather esoteric; many C++ programmers may never deal with them and may have no idea what they are. Exceptions are error conditions that are not expected to occur in normal processing. Consequently, they are not returned from a method as either arguments or the return value; nonetheless, they cannot be ignored. An example would be a method to compute the square root of a number. The normal interface expects a positive real number as an argument and returns a positive real number as a result. Since a program might incorrectly pass a negative number as an argument, the method can check for this and throw an exception when it occurs. In most systems, programmers are not required to deal with exceptions, and the occurrence of an unexpected exception causes abnormal program termination.

In Java, exceptions are a full-fledged part of the language. The signature of member functions includes exception information, and the language processor enforces a programming style whereby if you call a method that can throw an exception, you must check to see if any of the possible exceptions occurred and handle them. Almost every Java programmer will encounter exceptions, since some of the more-useful classes from the supplied libraries throw them. Dealing with exceptions is not difficult but is something you will need to be aware of. The documentation for a method must indicate the exceptions it throws. If you forget about them, don't worry; the compiler will remind you.

Strings are Different from Character Arrays in Java

Java includes a *String* object, which is a constant. A *String* is not the same as an array of characters, although it is easy to build a *String* object given an array of characters. You should use *String*s instead of arrays of characters wherever possible, as they cannot be overwritten by different values unintentionally.

Java has Limited Support for Constant Objects and Methods

In C++, you may declare a formal parameter to a function or a return value as *const*, effectively preventing the body of the function from modifying the argument and the caller from modifying the return value. In addition, you may declare a member function as constant, indicating it cannot change any aspect of the object upon which it operates.

Java supports the notion of constant, read-only values, using the *final* modifier. However, it does not support the notions of constraining writeable objects to be read only when passed as an argument, constraining return values to be read only, or constraining a method to not modify the object upon which it operates.

This omission is less of a problem in Java than it is in C++, mostly because of the differentiation between the *String* class and an array of characters, but it does leave a hole for errors. In particular, there is no way of ensuring that a method that should not modify an object does not inadvertently do so.

Java has no Pointers

Understanding the concept of pointers is one of the most difficult aspects of C and C++ programming. Pointers are also one of the biggest sources of errors. Java has no pointers; instead objects are passed as arguments directly, rather than passing pointers to objects. In addition, you must manipulate arrays using indices. Neither of these are a big deal in most cases; however, the lack of pointers is a major deal if you are writing systems where pointers to functions or pointers to member functions are involved. These situations arise frequently in systems involving callbacks with known signatures to objects of a base type, where numerous different methods having the same signature may all be used for a particular callback and are dynamically assigned. There are ways around the problem, but they are not particularly intuitive or convenient.

Java has no Parameterized Types

A parameterized type provides a means of writing one piece of code to describe an implementation for several similar types of arguments. An example would be a square-root method that operates on either integers or floating-point numbers. In C++, this capability is provided by templates.

Java has no equivalent of C++ templates. If you have been using templates merely as a convenience, such as to build several similar functions using different types of arguments (as in the previous example), this isn't too big a disaster. It means more cutting and pasting to write each of the similar classes or methods by hand, but does not present a serious roadblock in terms of whether or not you can write an equivalent program. However, if you have been using templates to automatically generate classes, it is a problem, and there is no easy way around it.

Java is Garbage Collected

In a garbage-collected language, the underlying run-time environment keeps track of which pieces of memory are in use and which are not. When a piece of memory is no longer needed, the system automatically reclaims the memory. For example, an object created inside a method, but not passed back to the caller or stored as part of a global object, can no longer be of any use after the method is exited. Call it magic if you like, but the system really does know which objects you are using, and which ones you can't possibly touch again because there are no references remaining that address them (this is one of the benefits of not having pointers in the language). As a result, you no longer need to worry about destroying objects when they are no longer in use or freeing memory returned by some function call. An incredible amount of time and debugging effort in C++ is focused on bugs caused by deleting objects which are still in use, or memory leaks caused by not deleting objects no longer in use. Java's use of garbage collection greatly reduces these errors, although it does not eliminate them—bad program logic can still leave no-longer-needed objects linked onto an active data structure, in which case they won't be garbage collected. Many classes in C++ contain destructors primarily to release auxiliary storage used by an object of the class. The fact that Java is garbage collected means you don't have to write destructors for these classes. It does not, however, mean you can forget about writing destructors for all classes. For example, an object that opens a network connection still needs to clean up gracefully by closing the connection when it is destroyed. In Java, a destructor is known as a "finalization method."

Java Does not Implement Multiple Inheritance

In any complex, object-oriented system, implementing a class that needs to inherit the functionality of more than one other class is a frequent problem. A *Manager* class, for example, might need to serve as the head of a linked list (of the employees the manager manages), but a *Manager* also needs to be an *Employee.* There are several ways of dealing with this problem. One of these is multiple inheritance—allowing a class to be derived from more than one base class. In this example, *Manager* could be derived from both *Linked List* and *Employee.*

Java does not implement multiple inheritance. Instead, you may declare interfaces, which describe the programming interface used to achieve some functionality. A class may then implement one or more interfaces, as well as its own unique functionality. Different, unrelated classes may implement the same interface. Formal parameters to methods may be declared as either classes or interfaces. If they are interfaces, objects of different classes that implement the interface may be passed as arguments to the method.

The concept of interfaces is considerably easier to master than multiple inheritance, but has its limitations. In particular, you must write code to reimplement the desired functionality in each class implementing an interface.

Java Supports Multithreading

Multithreading lets you write a program that potentially does two or more operations at the same time. For example, you could finish reading a large file while still allowing the user to edit the part already read in. To do this, you break your program into different threads of execution. To work correctly, the program needs to be careful about how the different threads manipulate any data or make decisions based on data common to more than one thread.

Java was designed to support multithreaded applications from the start. The classes and interfaces provided make breaking an application into different threads simple. Language primitives handle automatic synchronization and locking of critical data structures and methods.

Java Comes with a Diverse Set of Predefined Classes

The default Java environment currently consists of several different Java packages implementing a diverse set of fundamental classes. These give you a real jump start in terms of your ability to quickly write a meaningful application. They include the following:

java.awt. Most applications developed today make heavy reliance on GUIs. Java provides an abstract window toolkit (AWT), which allows you to deal with GUI objects in a generic manner without regard to the system on which your program is running. The big advantage is that your program will automatically run on all supported Java platforms. As of this writing, that includes Windows 95/NT and Sun UNIX platforms, but by the time you read this it will most likely include others, such as the Mac and most other UNIX flavors. The current awt is a least-common-denominator GUI toolkit, a problem not inherent in the Java design, but rather, a result of the rapid explosion of the technology, and time-to-market and resource constraints on the Java development team. Expect the AWT to evolve into a more full-functioned set of classes.

java.applet. An applet, in the context of Java, is a graphic piece of a larger program, focused primarily on providing some form of browser-related content. Applet itself is a subclass of an AWT component and provides extended capabilities to support rendering dynamic images, such as animations and audio.

java.io. The java.io package supplies classes to support reading and writing streams, files, and pipes.

java.lang. These classes support the basic Java objects and native types: Class, Object, Boolean, Float, Double, Integer, String, and so on, plus those dealing with the extended capabilities of the language and connection with the rest of the system environment.

java.net. The java.net package supplies classes to support network programming. These include dealing with sockets, Internet addresses, network datagrams, uniform resource locators (URLs), and content handlers for data from a URL.

java.util. These are general-purpose utility classes for data structures, such as dictionaries, hashtables, dates, stacks, bit sets, and strings. The package does not have the breadth of similar, commercial C++ libraries, but does provide convenient and time-saving implementations for some commonly needed classes.

Summary

Much of the popular press is claiming Java is much easier to learn than C++, heralding it as a breakthrough in that regard. Certain aspects of Java are easier to learn than C++, but the difficulties most people have in learning to program in both C++ and Java have little to do with the language itself. Instead, they have to do with fundamental, object-oriented concepts. If you understand those, picking up the Java syntax will be a breeze. If you don't, you will probably find Java just about as confusing as C++.

Porting Windows Applications to Java

Part I

Andrew Wilson

While much has been made of the similarities in syntax between C/C++ and Java, there are also a great many differences, especially in the overall approach to programming with the two languages. The lack of pointers and associated memory-management devices may leave even the hardiest C++ programmer at a loss concerning how to proceed. At the same time, scores of existing applications may be useful as Java applets or applications running on the Internet. These may be personal applications that you've written for your own use and want to make accessible to others from your home page, or they may be full-fledged commercial applications for which the Internet may represent a business opportunity. Either way, porting desktop applications to the Web is sure to become fashionable as Java support is standardized.

Andrew is an engineer at Nu Mega Technologies in Nashua, NH. Reprinted courtesy of Web Techniques.

```
DEFPUSHBUTTON "OK",IDOK,260,7,50,14

Button IDOK = new Button("OK");
```

Figure 1: *A default push putton, in both Windows and Java.*

In exploring this problem, I recently discovered a reasonably straightforward way of moving the user interface part of a C or C++ Windows application to Java. This article describes how you can take a Windows application, strip out the user interface, and place it into a Java class that runs as a Java applet without modification. In the process, I'll present the source code for a tool that automates the conversion. I'll also tell you about the Java Layout Manager, which presented one of the most difficult roadblocks to my task.

Windows Resource	Java Class
DEFPUSHBUTTON	Button
PUSHBUTTON	
LTEXT	Label
SCROLLBAR	Scrollbar
EDITTEXT	TextArea
	TextComponent
	TextField
LISTBOX	List
COMBOBOX	Choice
CONTROL	Checkbox
(check box, radio button)	

Table 1: *Windows resources and corresponding Java classes.*

Windows Resource Editor

Early Windows developers will remember how difficult it was to write a user interface for Windows applications. It seemed to take hours to build a resource script with all of the menu options, buttons, and dialog boxes. When compile time came, something was off just far enough to be annoying. So you'd have to go back and rework the user interface, taking still more time. Within five minutes of getting my first resource editor, I had created the same user interface that it had taken me hours to create the old, manual way.

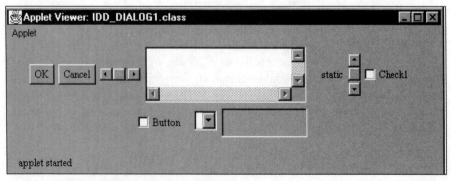

Figure 2: *The actual result of the porting process.*

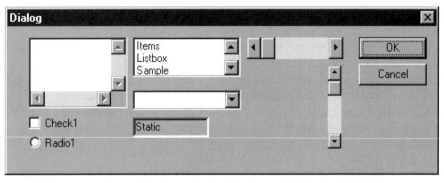

Figure 3: *The original Windows dialog box that was run through the resource-conversion tool.*

During my learning curve for Java, I concluded that one thing missing from the Java Development Kit was a resource editor. With Web browser in hand, I perused through several Java-related Web sites and found nothing like this to meet my needs. So I sat down and began to craft a tool that would give me the beginnings of just such a resource editor. The similarities between Windows and Java user-interface classes provided the key to this effort. The idea was to build a conversion tool that would take my Windows-application resource script and convert it into a Java initialization script within the *init()* section of an applet.

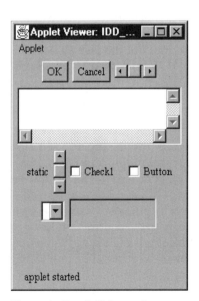

Figure 4: *Result if the applet window is made taller rather than wider.*

Java and Windows Controls

The first step in any conversion process is to examine just what controls are compatible. To my surprise, I discovered that for the most part, there is nothing in the user interface of a Windows application that cannot be done in a Java applet. There are a few things a Java applet can't do, and those are Windows-specific items that have no meaning beyond that platform. Table 1 shows a list of Windows controls and the corresponding Java classes that make up most of a user interface. This is a short list of the most commonly used controls. Both Java and Windows have many more possible items in the user-interface toolkit. In particular, Java is very impressive, with many possible interface choices a programmer can use. There are a total of

42 user-interface-related classes in Java, including layout managers, font and font metric classes, graphics, and windows.

With the list of convertible items in hand, the next step is to find out what information can be ignored and what is critical. Items such as load and memory options have no bearing on a Java class and can be ignored. The necessary items are the identifier for the resource, its X-Y location, width, height, and, in a few cases, the style parameters. Scroll bars, check boxes, edit boxes, and radio buttons are partially defined by their style and so are necessary, while items such as *LTEXT* have no corresponding styles and can safely be ignored in the conversion process.

The central problem in converting Windows resources to a Java class is knowing where to look for resources and how to define them in the target Java class. For example, the first line of the push-button definition in Figure 1 describes the button with the button identifier, the caption, a resource ID, width, and height. This line, short and sweet, defines exactly how and where the button should be rendered. In a Java applet, that line could be translated into the second line in Figure 1, which is all that is necessary to instantiate the button. In either case, some type of follow-up statement has to execute in order to actually draw the object on the screen. All converted resources would be recreated in this way.

The missing step is where to find these statements and how they are organized within a resource script. The *Dialog* keyword defines the dialog box that will be targeted and converted. Listing One shows the resource definition for a sample dialog box. In this example dialog resource, there are many things that can be ignored. The memory options, style, origin, caption, and font at the beginning of the resource definition are not necessary since the conversion process will create a Java applet with no comparable characteristics. The caption can be stored, but it is only for the application, not the Java applet. The important information lies between the *Begin* and *End* statements. My conversion tool will read in each resource, process it, convert it into a new Java class, and encapsulate it within the applet.

As stated earlier, some controls have special styles necessary to understand and process in order to create a proper corresponding Java class. *CONTROL* styles tell the type of control that should be created (though my tool will only convert to a *Checkbox*, since that is the only corresponding control in Java). Scroll bars have a default horizontal style, the *SBS_VERT* style, which must be trapped for the conversion.

Listing Two shows a converted resource file. The physical location of each control is not listed. This application merely recreates the control—it does not specify a layout. Layout is one of the most critical aspects of the conversion process. (I'll talk more about it later.) Each control retains its name rather than the value of its original definition. Also, duplicate types, such as the ever-present *IDC_STATIC*, are given names that are automatically incremented by one for each instance (the purpose of the present application is only to perform the conversion, not to provide better resource names). Once the conversion process is complete, the programmer can edit the applet by adding functions to bring the controls to life in order to make it far more useful than something that just displays buttons and edit boxes.

Listing Three shows the HTML code that can be used to display the converted Java applet. Of course, you can display this or any other converted applet in just about any type of HTML document you like, as long as it is viewed with a Java-enabled browser. However, there is a catch. If the current applet is included in an HTML page, it could be run, but not without a few unpredictable results.

After the porting process, the applet looks like Figure 2. It may, however, display somewhat differently because, as it exists, the Java code does not define a layout format. To get an idea of what I'm talking about, look at Figure 3, the original Windows dialog box that was run through the resource-conversion tool. Both dialog boxes have the same components, but there are significant differences. In effect, the conversion program converted the resources, but did not position them properly in the Java display area.

The Java-applet dialog box looks so different because of the differences in how a window is actually generated and displayed in the source and destination windowing environments. In Windows, resource coordinates are absolute. If the window is too small to show all of the controls, those controls are simply not displayed until the window is resized to be large enough to do so.

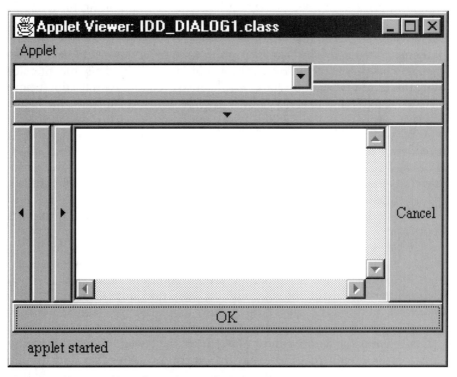

Figure 5: *The ported interface using* BorderLayout.

Applets written in Java are utterly different. Figure 4 shows what happens if the applet window is simply made taller rather than wider. The dialog box displayed to the user is completely different. Notice that all of the controls have been redistributed along the viewable interface. It doesn't matter if the dialog-box window is too small to show a given control; the Java layout manager will automatically redesign the applet interface so that it works on all target platforms. In retrospect, the reason it works this way is obvious. Java applets can't make any assumptions about the type of display system or desktop manager on which they will be running. Therefore, the Java layout manager has much greater control over the organization and appearance of the applet than in a typical desktop manager.

The Java Layout Manager

There are five different methods of laying out controls in a Java applet, none of which convert directly into the absolute X-Y coordinates used by Windows resources. Obviously, this puts a real crimp into the idea of a straightforward utility that converts from a Windows interface, which is entirely X-Y governed, into a world of free-floating objects. Each layout type provides a slightly different effect.

The first layout type is the *BorderLayout*. When an object is actually added to the interface, the location is also given. The location is either *North*, *South*, *East*, *West*, or *Center*. Figure 5 shows the interface using this layout. Again we see an interface that does not look very much like the original Windows interface. There is a better way to organize it, however. Each cell can have a new panel or container added to it. The container can then hold the various controls, creating a much better user interface, as shown in Figure 6. Suddenly the interface using this layout type almost looks usable. It still requires modification before it is identical to the original Windows interface. Listing Four shows the modified Java output that produced this interface.

Another type of layout is the *FlowLayout*. This uses a simple technique when it renders a display. There are three parameters to *FlowLayout—Center*, *Right*, *and Left*—which determine how it will position the controls. This layout type uses the same concept as a word processor, which positions text left-justified, right-justified, or centered.

With *GridLayout*, the controls are laid out in a grid fashion. *GridLayout* starts in the upper left-hand corner of the window and works its way to the lower right. *GridLayout* works either across the rows of down the columns, depending on how it was initialized. When it finishes a row or column, it moves on to the next one. *GridBagLayout* is a more powerful version of *GridLayout* that allows each cell to be a different size. The cells are laid out the same as with *GridLayout*, but there is a much greater ability to manage the placement of controls.

CardLayout is the last and most powerful of the layout options. *CardLayout* allows cards of controls to be stacked on top of each other and flipped through, just as you would with a deck of playing cards. So a single button could exist on Card 1, for example, an edit box on Card 2, and a *GridLayout* of a calculator on Card 3. A set of controls outside of the *CardLayout* could be used to flip through the cards so that a user may select which control to use.

How the Application Works

My resource-conversion application is not terribly complex. It is written in Visual C++ 4.1 and runs on Windows NT or Windows 95. It also uses the Microsoft Foundation Classes (MFC) to build the user interface and do all the file I/O. The resource-conversion utility first asks the user to select a file from a pop-up dialog box. Once the file has been selected, the program will parse the file and read everything except for the header files. It ignores the header files because, as you may remember, they contain definitions not used in the Java applet. Since we use the definition identifier of a control as the control's new name, we no longer need its value. Several keywords are simply ignored, such as the *#if* series. The additional code included with such statements is not really necessary. If two dialogs appear within an *#ifdef*, the conversion application parses and handles both.

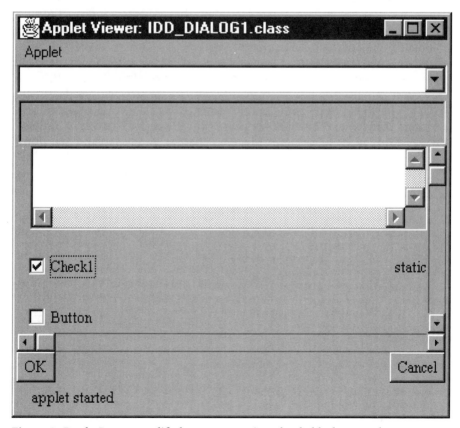

Figure 6: BorderLayout *modified to use a container that holds the controls.*

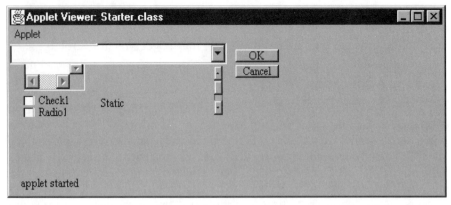

Figure 7: *The result of using* setLayout(null) *rather than one of the five layout types provided.*

When the parse occurs, the resulting construct is also syntax-checked against a syntax definition for that keyword. If the line is valid, it is translated into its base components of name, caption, type, X-Y coordinates, height and width, and any special styles. The application then adds this information to a derived *CList* object that contains the main dialog information and stores a list of all controls.

After parsing, the user may select from a list box which dialog window to export. The export process builds a generic Java class. It will create the class and generate the minimum to create a Java user interface. This leads us back to the layout manager, discussed a little earlier.

At first glance, it seems that any work with the control layout is complex, and the result is not always immediately apparent. In particular, none of the defined layout types produce a user interface that corresponds to that of the original Windows X-Y coordinate. The solution has to do with the *setLayout*

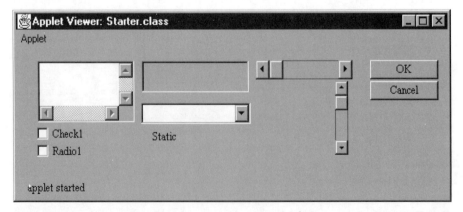

Figure 8: *The reformatted dialog box.*

call, shown in Listing Four. *setLayout* lets you designate which layout type you want to use to position controls on your application.

What isn't so obvious is that there is a sixth layout type. This type will allow us to place objects anywhere within the Java applet using real X-Y coordinates. It is not documented, but nothing says that we can't do this. Instead of using a layout manager in *setLayout*, use the *null* designation. The line *setLayout(null)* results in no layout manager being used, giving us X-Y mapping ability.

Figure 7 shows the effect of using *setLayout(null)* and the resulting X-Y locations listed in the Windows resource script. It looks similar to the original, but everything is noticeably smaller, the combo box is at the top of the screen, and the list box is nowhere to be seen.

Let's first address the problem of the smaller environment. Windows does not actually use real X-Y coordinates in a dialog box; instead it uses Dialog Logical Units (DLUs). DLUs are based upon the selected font. The horizontal DLU is equal to the value of the font's average width divided by 4. The vertical DLU is equal to the value of the font's average height divided by 8. In the sample script, 8 point MS Sans Serif was used. Its actual DLU is 1.75×2. Java uses X-Y coordinates based on pixels. To convert from DLUs to pixels, we simply use the ratio of 1/DLU, which will give us the real pixel conversion. So for the horizontal conversion we have a value of .57 (1/1.75) and a vertical of .50 (1/2). We must add 57 percent to every X coordinate and 50 percent to each Y coordinate.

The next problem is that of the combo and list boxes. These two objects don't like to be reshaped, so you wrap a layout manager around the individual objects and reshape the panel. Figure 8 shows the reformatted dialog box, which is nearly identical to the original. Listing Five shows the new source code. The code has changed a bit from the other examples. The declarations for all the controls (except for their panels) are now member declarations. This allows an event handler to be added that lets a user interact with the controls.

The Journey Begins

Interestingly enough, this same strategy can be used to port Windows resource files (or the resource file of any user interface) to any object-oriented language and environment. I've already written a companion application that ports the Windows resource files to MFC classes. This porting tool can be used to take the user interfaces of existing Windows applications and port them into the 32-bit Windows environment using MFC.

A slightly different tool will have to be developed for every type of source resource file (Windows, X, Macintosh, and so on) and the corresponding object-oriented class structure (MFC, COM, CORBA, and OpenDoc). Fortunately, there are only a few of each, and once this activity is completed, any number of user interfaces can be converted to object classes.

While this does not make porting the entire application a snap, it works very well for the application's user interface. This makes it possible to deliver the same look and feel between Windows and Java, or even to design the user interface using one of the many available Windows resource editors, and port it cleanly to Java. The uses are virtually unlimited.

Listing One

```
IDD_DIALOG1 DIALOG DISCARDABLE 0, 0, 317, 95
STYLE DS_MODALFRAME | WS_POPUP | WS_CAPTION | WS_SYSMENU
CAPTION "Dialog"
FONT 8, "MS Sans Serif"
BEGIN
        DEFPUSHBUTTON        "OK",IDOK,260,7,50,14
        PUSHBUTTON          "Cancel", IDCANCEL,260,24,50,14
        SCROLLBAR             IDC_SCROLLBAR1,177,7,71,14
        EDITTEXT              IDC_EDIT1,16,7,73,46,ES_MULTILINE |
                              WS_VSCROLL | WS_HSCROLL
        LTEXT                 "Static",IDC_STATIC,93,59,56,13,SS_SUNKEN |
                              WS_BORDER
        SCROLLBAR             IDC_SCROLLBAR2,237,25,10,54,SBS_VERT
        CONTROL
                        "Check1",IDC_CHECK1,"Button",BS_AUTOCHECKBOX |
                              WS_TABSTOP,16,58,54,10
        CONTROL             BS_AUTORADIOBUTTON,16, 71,49,10
        COMBOBOX            IDC_COMBO1,93,41,80,26,CBS_DROPDOWN |
                              CBS_SORT | WS_VSCROLL | WS_TABSTOP
        LISTBOX             IDC_LIST1,93,7,79,26,LBS_SORT |
                              LBS_NOINTEGRALHEIGHT | WS_VSCROLL |
                              WS_TABSTOP
END
```

Listing Two

```
import java.util.*;
import java.applet.*;
import java.awt.*;


public class IDD_DIALOG1 extends Applet
{

        public void init()
        {
        // add layout method

                Button IDOK = new Button("OK");
                add(IDOK);

                Button IDCANCEL = new Button("Cancel");
                add(IDCANCEL);

                Scrollbar IDC_SCROLLBAR1 =new Scrollbar(Scrollbar.HORIZONTAL);
                add(IDC_SCROLLBAR1);
```

```
                     TextArea IDC_EDIT1 = new TextArea(""3,30);
                     add(IDC_EDIT1);

                     Label IDC_STATIC = new Label("static");
                     add(IDC_STATIC);

                     Scrollbar IDC_SCROLLBAR2 = new Scrollbar(Scrollbar.VERTICAL);
                     add(IDC_SCROLLBAR2);

                     Checkbox IDC_CHECK1 = new Checkbox("Check1");
                     add(IDC_CHECK1);

                     Checkbox IDC_RADIO1 = new Checkbox("Button");
                     add(IDC_RADIO1);

                     Choice IDC_COMBO1 = new Choice();
                     add(IDC_COMBO1);

                     List IDC_LIST1 = new List(2,false);
                     add(IDC_LIST1);


             }
}
```

Listing Three

```
<HTML>
<HEAD>
<TITLE>Converted Applet User Interface</TITLE>
</HEAD>
<BODY>
<H1>
OK, Here we go!
</H1>
<P>
Getting ready to load converted applet.
<APPLET CODE = IDD_DIALOG1.class WIDTH=500 HEIGHT=400>
</APPLET>

<P>
</BODY>
</HTML>
```

Listing Four

```
import java.util.*;
import java.applet.*;
import java.awt.*;


public class IDD_DIALOG1 extends Applet
{
```

```java
Panel North;
Panel South;
Panel East;
Panel West;
Panel Center;
public void init()
{
        setLayout(new BorderLayout());
        Center = new Panel();
        West = new Panel();
        East = new Panel();
        South = new Panel();
        North = new Panel();

        add("North",North);
        add("South",South);
        add("East",East);
        add("West",West);
        add("Center",Center);

        South.setLayout(new BorderLayout());
        Center.setLayout(new BorderLayout());
        East.setLayout(new BorderLayout());
        West.setLayout(new BorderLayout());
        North.setLayout(new BorderLayout());

        Button IDOK = new Button("OK");
        South.add("West",IDOK);

        Button IDCANCEL = new Button("Cancel");
        South.add("East",IDCANCEL);

        Scrollbar IDC_SCROLLBAR1 =new Scrollbar(Scrollbar.HORIZONTAL);
        South.add("North",IDC_SCROLLBAR1);

        TextArea IDC_EDIT1 = new TextArea("",3,30);
        Center.add("North",IDC_EDIT1);

        Label IDC_STATIC = new Label("static");
        Center.add("East",IDC_STATIC);

        Scrollbar IDC_SCROLLBAR2 = new Scrollbar(Scrollbar.VERTICAL);
        East.add("West",IDC_SCROLLBAR2);

        Checkbox IDC_CHECK1 = new Checkbox("Check1");
        Center.add("Center",IDC_CHECK1);

        Checkbox IDC_RADIO1 = new Checkbox("Button");
        Center.add("South",IDC_RADIO1);

        Choice IDC_COMBO1 = new Choice();
        North.add("North",IDC_COMBO1);

        List IDC_LIST1 = new List(2,false);
```

```
                North.add("Center",IDC_LIST1);


        }
}
```

Listing Five

```
import java.util.*;
import java.applet.*;
import java.awt.*;


public class Starter extends Applet
{

        Button IDOK;
        Button IDCANCEL;
        Scrollbar IDC_SCROLLBAR1;
        TextArea IDC_EDIT1;
        Label IDC_STATIC;
        Scrollbar IDC_SCROLLBAR2;
        Checkbox IDC_CHECK1;
        Checkbox IDC_RADIO1;
        Choice IDC_COMBO1;
        List IDC_LIST1;

        public void init()
        {
                setLayout(null);

                IDOK = new Button("OK");
                IDOK.reshape(408,14,78,21);
                add(IDOK);

                IDCANCEL = new Button("Cancel");
                IDCANCEL.reshape(408,37,78,21);
                add(IDCANCEL);

                IDC_SCROLLBAR1 = new Scrollbar(Scrollbar.HORIZONTAL);
                IDC_SCROLLBAR1.reshape(277,14,111,21);
                add(IDC_SCROLLBAR1);

                IDC_EDIT1 = new TextArea("",3,30);
                IDC_EDIT1.reshape(25,14,114,69);
                add(IDC_EDIT1);

                IDC_STATIC = new Label("Static");
                IDC_STATIC.reshape(146,88,87,19);
                add(IDC_STATIC);

                IDC_SCROLLBAR2 = new Scrollbar(Scrollbar.VERTICAL);
                IDC_SCROLLBAR2.reshape(368,37,15,81);
                add(IDC_SCROLLBAR2);
```

```
            IDC_CHECK1 = new Checkbox("Check1");
            IDC_CHECK1.reshape(25,87,100,15);
            add(IDC_CHECK1);

            IDC_RADIO1 = new Checkbox("Radio1");
            IDC_RADIO1.reshape(25,106,76,15);
            add(IDC_RADIO1);

            IDC_COMBO1 = new Choice();
            Panel IDC_COMBO1PANEL = new Panel();
            IDC_COMBO1PANEL.reshape(146,61,125,39);
            IDC_COMBO1PANEL.setLayout(new GridLayout(1,1,1,1));
            IDC_COMBO1PANEL.add(IDC_COMBO1);
            add(IDC_COMBO1PANEL);

            IDC_LIST1 = new List(2,false);
            Panel IDC_LIST1PANEL = new Panel();
            IDC_LIST1PANEL.setLayout(new GridLayout(1,1,1,1));
            IDC_LIST1PANEL.reshape(146,14,124,39);
            IDC_LIST1PANEL.add(IDC_LIST1);
            add(IDC_LIST1PANEL);
        }
    }
```

End Listings

Porting Windows Applications to Java

Part II

Andrew Wilson

In Part I, I examined the difficulties of compatibility and conversion of Windows user interfaces to Java. There were differences in the layout of the user interfaces, first in the appropriate layout manager to use and second in the conversion from DLUs (Dialog Logical Units) to pixels. However, there was nothing that really couldn't be overcome.

In Part II, I look at how to write a translation utility that can move a Windows user interface to a Java class. The idea of a conversion utility to translate one resource type to another application or platform is very appealing. It doesn't have to be limited to converting a Windows resource script to a Java applet; it could be modified to convert a Visual Basic form to a Windows resource script or to a Java applet.

Andrew is an engineer at Nu Mega Technologies in Nashua, NH. Reprinted courtesy of Web Techniques.

Creating a tool to convert one development environment to another is not really hard. Creating it so that it can be quickly updated, difficult to crash, and robust enough to deal with syntax and language independence is much more tricky. The issue is not one of programming, but one of design.

Requirements for the Porting Utility

To start, let's think about what we'll need to do the work. First, we know we need a parser. The parser for my utility supports only Windows resource scripts, but it will become apparent how it is modified to support any source language. Second, we need some type of language generator to be responsible for producing the Java code. The trick is to keep the parser and the generator separate. To this end, I create an intermediate linked list of elements that will contain only the information the generator needs.

It may not be very clear why an intermediate layer should be used. When we look at a spoken language, we often find odd things in syntax that become all too apparent during translation. In some languages, there are special suffixes and prefixes for male and female nouns. In others, the syntactical conversion might change the order of some words. Many statements don't translate well. A direct translation from a given language might be "I to the beach drive," while the actual translation would be "I drive to the beach." The intermediate layer of the application is the direct translation, a state where it may not be syntactically correct, but contains enough information to be accurately converted to the actual translation.

The result is an interesting idea. The source language and the target language are irrelevant, as long as they both understand the intermediate translation. Once we know this, there is no reason why the application couldn't be modified to convert any resource file to a target object class or resource language. The tool will convert any dialog resource-script block into an intermediate state, which can then be interpreted to generate the final code.

Next is to find a way to convert the resource script into some generic form. This is commonly done using a parser, but before we can even write the parser we need to make a few assumptions about the incoming resource script. The first—and most important—assumption is that the incoming resource script has no syntactical errors. This tool is supposed to assist in the conversion of an application from one platform to another. This implies that there is a working copy of the application on a given platform.

The second assumption is that we don't care about preprocessor directives. This may sound a little frightening to an experienced programmer, so let me explain. The preprocessor directives determine what exactly gets compiled based upon what preprocessor settings were made for a given build. We could simulate this, or we could just convert everything and let the person using the translator figure out which to use. The latter is much easier to implement, by eliminating every *pragma* and *IF*-type statement in the script. We could translate menus, bitmaps, icons, and string tables, but we won't at this time. Extra options would triple the size of the parser class, and can be added easily later on.

The Parser Operation

The next step is to figure out a way to work through the incoming resource data and convert it to an intermediate state. To start, I'll search for a given set of keywords line by line through the resource file. The program will create a keyword list initialized with all the keywords we are interested in using. When we search a line, I'll just load the line and do a string search for the keyword. If the keyword is found, a second-stage parser will start and continue the parse. This is the first-stage parser.

The second-stage parser will break the line into a set of standalone words, which were separated by commas and spaces in the original resource file. These are the only two items we will base the parsing on. The only exception would have been parentheses, but these are typically found in expressions that are part of *IF* statements, which we don't process.

The second stage will also create two lists. The first will contain token and item information; the second will store strings and identifiers. A token will be a numeric representation for the type of word being processed. Tokens will represent things like identifiers, keywords, controls, strings, styles, and integers. Each token will be followed by an integer, with the token determining the following integer. For example, identifier and string tokens will be followed by an integer that points to the index in the string list where the identifier is stored. Keyword tokens are followed by the index of the keyword in the keyword list. An *Integer* keyword is followed by the integer. Styles will also be followed with the numeric representation of the style. Controls, as with keywords, are followed by the index of the control keyword.

The parser must support two layers of keywords. For example, *DIALOG* defines an organization of controls. A secondary keyword is a control such as *EDITTEXT*, which is encapsulated within *DIALOG* constructs. The control keywords will be in a list of all the keywords that would normally be encapsulated within a *DIALOG* construct.

Stage two will parse until it hits either an *END* word or end of file. If end of file is reached, an error state is generated and the translation fails. This is because the keywords we'll be working with must be terminated by an *END* statement.

Other items will simply be ignored until the next keyword, such as *STYLE*. We'll simply ignore everything from the keyword *STYLE* until we reach the next keyword, whatever that might be. Ignored keywords and their parameters are not added to the token list or the string list. This means we must create a third list of keywords, those to be ignored.

There are also parameters that have to be ignored, to be placed in yet another list. Anything that should be ignored is bypassed, and we move on to the next word. Unlike the above keyword list, these parameters are only ignored for that instance, but the remainder of the parameters are read and processed.

Stage three of the parse will move the lists of tokens and strings into a series of links in a list. A single linked list is used to store the controls for a given dialog. As each token is read, a different control grabber is used for each control. The control grabber knows what order each parameter is supposed to be in. When a parameter is not found where it is supposed to be, then an error state is generated. Otherwise each control is added to the link list with the appropriate parameters attached to it. Also, the conversion from DLU to pixel layout occurs here.

When stage three has finished, the link list is added to a link list of dialogs. When the application has completely parsed the resource file, the user may have several dialogs in a single list, each displayed in a list box. The user simply selects which dialog he or she wishes to convert from the list, and then clicks on the Export button.

At that point, the translator activates the Java-language generator. It receives the dialog control list the user selected. Each item is read from the list twice: Once to build the declaration for the each control, and a second time to initialize the control.

There are two steps to this. First, the Java-class generator executes, which creates the declaration for the applet. As a part of its execution, it calls the identifier function, which creates the control declarations and returns. Then the initialization function is called, which creates the *init()* code for the applet. It will generate the control initializers into the *init()* code block and return. The class generator then closes the applet and returns to the main application.

A Closer Look at the Parser Lists

It should be apparent that the application could be converted to translate nearly any resource script from one platform to another rather easily. Now let's look at a few key code sections. The entire application is written in C++, which means that as long as your class returns the intermediate state information correctly, you can replace the code of the parse class to parse the resources of any platform into something readable by the Java output class.

The complete source is available on the CD-ROM, along with the executable application. The application was written and tested under Visual C++ 4.1. Be aware that the application is very memory intensive, since simplicity was an important factor in its design.

Let's look at some of the lists we are working with. They are, sadly, very big arrays. I did this only because making it more memory efficient would just expand the code too much. Even now, there are over a thousand lines of code. Listing One shows the list declarations.

m_lpszKeywordList contains the Keywords. There are only two, but more can be added as needed. This is a list for the first stage of the parser. *m_lpsz-ControlList* holds all the normal controls that would be encapsulated in the above keyword constructs. There are only a few for this example, but they can be expanded to deal with many more. Further, this list contains the few styles that are useful to us (*SBS_VERT, BS_AUTOCHECKBOX, BS_AUTORA-DIOBUTTON*). This is a list for the second stage of the parser.

m_lpszIgnoreList are the modifiers in a keyword construct that we don't care about, such as *STYLE, CAPTION* and *FONT*. By avoiding them, we can clean out the extra words that do not add value to the intermediate layer. Any item listed here will cause the parser to ignore everything until it reaches an item in the *m_lpszControlList*. This is also a second-stage list.

m_lpszIgnoreParamList is massive; it holds 102 items and was the only list with which I tried to reduce the memory requirements. It serves a type of clean-up function. Parameters such as *SS_BORDER* are useless and can't be converted to a Java class. Normally I would just ignore the entry and continue, but *SS_BORDER* could be confused as an identifier, so it became necessary to create this list, which causes the greatest slowdown in the code. You will note in its particular code listing that it is very different from the other search functions. It is run against everything that is not caught in the previous lists. Again, this is a second-stage list.

m_IgnoreListLens will store the lengths of the items in the other lists. The previous list is also run through a simple bubble sort to create a list of items from smallest to longest. The *m_Ignore-ListLens* is used to help speed the search algorithm. The impact of this improved the speed of the search by more than 50 percent.

m_TokenList and *m_StringList* store everything that was parsed. *m_TokenList* holds the list of tokens after each object is parsed. Listing Two shows the actual token list, consisting of *#define* statements. Note that they are all powers of two, because it is possible to create a much more powerful syntax checker than the one I included. A syntax definition could be added for each keyword and control to create a syntax list. *I_TYPE* is used for keyword, the others are pretty apparent. *I_DONE* is used to represent an end of construct, usually terminated with an *END* statement. We will see these definitions used throughout the application.

Listing Three shows the Stage 1 parser. It loads a single line of resource-file information, strips out C++-style comments (// comments only, not the older, C-style /* */ constructs), checks if it contains an item from the keyword list and, if so, executes the Stage 2 parse. If Stage 2 is successful, it moves to Stage 3.

Before we look at *ItemType*, let's take a short look at the Stage 2 parser, as seen in Listing Four. It first parses the line passed to it, and then parses the remainder of the block or file if there is no end statement in the construct. *ParseLine* actually breaks the line into a set of words and fills the token and string lists. Table 1 shows a sample of what a token list may look like. When any item is converted, it looks similar to this. The ignore lists make it easy to keep just the important information in the token and string lists.

Listing Five shows the *ItemType, GetType*, and *IgnoreParamType* functions. *ItemType* returns a keyword. Note that the sort method is dynamic. If you want to add a keyword, just add it to the list and *ItemType* will still return the correct value. Further, the *ParseLine* function (not shown) works based on the return value of *ItemType*, so it is easy to extend the constructs supported by adding them to the existing construct logic.

GetType checks the keyword against all known types and if it finds nothing, it assumes that the item must be an identifier. If the item is not an identifier and should be ignored, add it to either the ignore or ignore-parameter lists. *Ignore-ParamType* uses a series of tests to see if the item exists in the list by first matching the size of the word to the size of the word in the ignore-parameter list. It then tests to see if it has found the actual word and returns.

The syntax checker (Listing Six) is relatively crude. If things aren't exactly where they are supposed to be, the checker fails and returns. The checker uses offsets in the token list to find the token type. It only checks to make sure the token is exactly where it is supposed to be. Tokens are always on an even-numbered index, while values are always odd.

This is not the best way to implement a syntax checker, but in this version, it is fast and fits the level of syntax checking we need to run with. Since we know what offset everything is at in relation to the keyword, we can test for the location of various types to confirm they exist where they are supposed to. There is no real way to trick the syntax checker into allowing an illegal construct. Once the syntax check is complete, the values of the types are passed into storage values, which are then passed into the constructor for an individual *CItem* class, shown in Listing Seven. This object is added to a *CDialogBlock* (derived *CObList*) object.

We can also see that the conversion from DLU to pixel layout occurs here. It must happen here, because there is no other location in the application that could be aware of the position of the X, Y, width, and height variables.

TOKEN VALUE	VALUE STORED	EXPLANATION
I_IDENTIFIER	0	An identifier was found and its text representation is stored in index 0 of the string array.
I_TYPE	0	The DIALOG keyword was found
I_VALUE	3	An integer with a value of 3
I_VALUE	0	An integer with a value of 0
I_VALUE	60	An integer with a value of 60
I_VALUE	234	An integer with a value of 234

Table 1: *A sample token list created by the parser.*

Conclusion

These functions represent the heart of the parser. The Java-class generator simply streams through the dialog-item linked list and builds the corresponding Java class. It is obvious how it works from the source code.

Building on this Foundation

As we can see, a porting utility like this is still wide open for expansion and improvement. Functionality to convert between many platforms is not beyond the reach of this simple tool, which was designed so that a new keyword or even a new language could be incorporated with minimal effort.

Java is quickly becoming a serious development platform. With that, new porting tools will need to be built and, in turn, old applications will get ported. Porting tools are few and far between. By getting in on the porting-tool market now, there is a strong possibility of having a product ready to go to market by the time Java is well established. That helps not just the utility's developer, but the entire Java-applet market.

Listing One

```
char m_lpszKeywordList[20][20];
char m_lpszControlList[20][20];
char m_lpszIgnoreList[20][20];
char m_lpszIgnoreParamList[105][35];
int m_IgnoreListLens[105];
char m_StringList[5000];
int m_TokenList[2000];
```

Listing Two

```
#define I_STRING        1
#define I_VALUE         2
#define I_TYPE          4
#define I_OPTIONAL              8
#define I_DONE  16
#define I_CONTROL               32
#define I_IGNORE        64
#define I_IDENTIFIER            128
#define I_IGNOREPARAM   256
```

Listing Three

```
BOOL CResourceFile::Stage1(void)
{
// Search file for keyword DIALOG or DIALOGEX

        CString strLine;
        while(GetLine(strLine)){
                if(strLine.Find("//") != -1)
```

```
                    strLine = strLine.Left(strLine.GetLength() -
(strLine.GetLength() - strLine.Find("//")));

               if(ItemType(strLine))
                if(!Stage2(strLine))
                        Stage3();

               m_TokenPointer = 0;
               m_StringListCount = 0;
               }
return TRUE;
}
```

Listing Four

```
BOOL CResourceFile::Stage2(CString& strLine){
      if(!ParseLine(strLine))
             return FALSE;

      while(GetLine(strLine))
             if(!ParseLine(strLine))
              return FALSE;

      return TRUE;
}
```

Listing Five

```
BOOL CResourceFile::ItemType(CString strWord){
      if(GetKeyword(strWord) != -1)
              return TRUE;
      return FALSE;
}

BOOL CResourceFile::IgnoreType(CString strWord){
      if(strWord.GetLength() == 0)
             return FALSE;
      CString strTemp;
      for(int wCounter = 0;wCounter < m_IgnoreListCount;wCounter++){
             if((UINT)strWord.GetLength() !=
             (UINT)strlen(m_lpszIgnoreList[wCounter]))
              strTemp = Spaced(m_lpszIgnoreList[wCounter]);
             else
              strTemp = m_lpszIgnoreList[wCounter];
             if(strWord.Find(strTemp) != -1)
              return TRUE;
      }
      return FALSE;
}
int CResourceFile::GetKeyword(CString strWord){
      if(strWord.GetLength() == 0)
              return -1;
      CString strTemp;
```

```
        for(int wCounter = 0;wCounter < m_KeywordListCount;wCounter++){
                if((UINT)strWord.GetLength() !=
                (UINT)strlen(m_lpszKeywordList[wCounter]))
                 strTemp = Spaced(m_lpszKeywordList[wCounter]);
                else
                 strTemp = m_lpszKeywordList[wCounter];
                if(strWord.Find(strTemp) != -1)
                 return wCounter;
        }
        return -1;
}
int CResourceFile::GetType(CString strWord){
        if(StringType(strWord))
                return I_STRING;

        if(ControlType(strWord))
                return I_CONTROL;

        if(ItemType(strWord))
                return I_TYPE;

        if(ValueType(strWord))
                return I_VALUE;

        if(IgnoreType(strWord))
                return I_IGNORE;

        if(EndofBlock(strWord))
                return I_DONE;

        if(IgnoreParamType(strWord))
                return I_IGNOREPARAM;

return I_IDENTIFIER;
}
```

Listing Six

```
if(m_TokenList[m_TokenPointer+2] != I_STRING)
       return FALSE;
if(m_TokenList[m_TokenPointer+4] != I_IDENTIFIER)
return FALSE;
if(m_TokenList[m_TokenPointer+6] != I_VALUE)
       return FALSE;
if(m_TokenList[m_TokenPointer+8] != I_VALUE)
       return FALSE;
if(m_TokenList[m_TokenPointer+10] != I_VALUE)
       return FALSE;
if(m_TokenList[m_TokenPointer+12] != I_VALUE)
       return FALSE;
Caption = m_StringList+m_TokenList[m_TokenPointer+3];
Id = m_StringList+m_TokenList[m_TokenPointer+5];
x = m_TokenList[m_TokenPointer+7] * 1.57;
y = m_TokenList[m_TokenPointer+9] * 1.50;
```

```
width = m_TokenList[m_TokenPointer+11] * 1.57;
height = m_TokenList[m_TokenPointer+13] * 1.50;
special = 0;
m_TokenPointer += 14;
```

Listing Seven

```
class CItem: public CObject
{
public:
      CString ID;
      CString Caption;
      int ItemType;
      int X;
      int Y;
      int Width;
      int Height;
      int Special;
public:
      CItem(){};
      CItem(CString id, CString caption,int type,int x,int y, int width, int
            height, int special):
      ID(id), Caption(caption), ItemType(type), X(x), Y(y), Width(width),
      Height(height), Special(special)
      {};
};
```

End Listings

The Java and C Connection

Anil Hemrajani

In recent months, one of the hottest technologies to hit the streets has been Java. It has taken the information systems industry by such a storm that most software vendors have jumped on the bandwagon to develop products for Java. Meanwhile, many companies still have large investments in applications written in other languages, such as C. My goal here is to show you how to interface to C from Java. I assume that you have a working knowledge of both Java and C.

Java provides a native method interface which can be used to invoke functions written in other languages. Currently only an interface to C is supported. (Of course, C++ source code can be accessed via C functions). There are approximately six steps required for connecting a Java program to C. The two main steps include writing the Java program and C functions. The remaining steps are required for gluing the two together.

Here is a simple example to illustrate each of these six steps. The example consists of a Java program that calls a C function to print the message "Hello Java" (a twist on the typical "Hello World" message). To keep the first example simple, no parameters are passed to the C function and no values are returned from it. Figure 1 provides a visual representation of the various components created from the following six steps required to make the Java and C connection:

Anil currently provides software engineering and training consulting services to a Fortune 500 corporation in McLean, VA. He can be contacted at anil@patriot.net or via http://www.patriot.net/users/anil/. Reprinted courtesy of C/C++ Users Journal.

1. Write a Java program.

2. Compile it.

3. Generate a header file for the C function.

4. Generate a stub file for the C function.

5. Write the C function.

6. Build a dynamic link library with the C function.

Let's look at each of these steps in more detail.

Step 1

The following is a simple Java program that defines a native method SayHi. Its implementation is provided in step 5:

```
public class HelloJava
{
    public native void SayHi();

    public static void
        main(String args[])
    {
    System.loadLibrary("hello");
    new HelloJava().SayHi();
    }
}
```

Native methods are declared much the same way as regular Java methods, with two differences. The declaration must contain the *native* keyword, and there is no body for the method in Java. The body is provided in the C function. The *loadLibrary* method (part of the Java *System* class) must be called prior to using the native method so that the dynamic link library containing the C function can be loaded. The *new* expression must be used to instantiate a native method.

What I have just shown here is one way of instantiating a native method. Alternatively, the native method could be declared in another Java class. In that case, we instantiate that Java class using a *new* expression, then simply call the native method off of the class. This style is used in Listing 3 and described below.

Step 2

Compile the Java class using a Java compiler, such as javac utility provided with the Java Development Kit (JDK). Running the following command will generate a Java byte code file, *HelloJava.class*:

```
javac HelloJava.java
```

Step 3

Generate a header file for the C function using the javah utility. The generated header file (*HelloJava.h*) basically provides a prototype for the C function, which is covered in step 5.

```
javah HelloJava
```

Step 4

Generate a stub function, using the javah utility, to connect the Java class to the C function. The following command will generate a stub file named *HelloJava.c*:

```
javah -stubs HelloJava
```

Step 5

Provide an implementation for the C function, *SayHi*:

```
/* HelloJavaImp.c: Implementation of
   Java native method, SayHi(). */
#include "HelloJava.h"
#include <stdio.h>

void HelloJava_SayHi(struct HHelloJava *javaObj)
{
    printf("Hello Java!\n");
}
```

Three things in the above source code deserve mention. First, the header file generated in step 3, *HelloJava.h*, must be included in the C module. Second, notice the name of the C function, *HelloJava_SayHi*. It contains the name of the Java class and the native method separated by an underscore. You will come across this naming convention (*class_method*) whenever you are interfacing with native methods in Java.

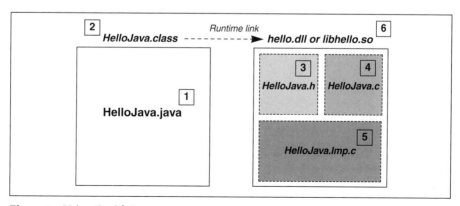

Figure 1: *Using C with Java.*

Last, an automatic parameter is always passed as the first parameter to a native method. It is essentially a handle to the Java class invoking the native method. You can think of this parameter as the *this* keyword in C++. I discuss how to use this parameter below.

Step 6

Build a dynamic link library. Here is a simple makefile which contains targets for building a dynamic link library on Windows 95, using the Microsoft C/C++ compiler, and a shared library on Solaris. The environment variable *JAVAHOME* points to the root directory of the JDK:

```
all:
    @echo Please specify a target: Win95 or Sun.

Win95:
    cl HelloJavaImp.c HelloJava.c \
-I$(JAVAHOME)\include -I$(JAVAHOME)\include\win32 \
-Fehello.dll -MD -LD $(JAVAHOME)\lib\javai.lib

Sun:
    cc -G -I$(JAVAHOME)/include -I$(JAVAHOME)/include/solaris \
HelloJavaImp.c HelloJava.c -o libhello.so
```

Once you have completed the above six steps successfully, you are ready to run the sample Java and C application. Here is how you would test the application and the output you should receive:

```
C:\ANIL\Doc\Articles\Java-C\Example1> java HelloJava
Hello Java!
```

Passing Parameters and Returning Values

Now that I have shown you the basic steps required to connect Java programs to C functions, it is time to get a little fancier by passing parameters to a C function and returning values from it. Since steps 2, 3, 4 and 6 are similar for all cases, I concentrate on steps 1 and 5 which deal with a Java program and C function(s), respectively. But before plunging into the specifics of these examples, I provide a quick overview of Java data types and how they correspond to C data types.

The following table provides a list of Java native data types and their machine sizes:

Type	Size
byte	8-bit
char	16-bit
short	16-bit
int	32-bit
float	32-bit
long	64-bit
double	64-bit

As you might notice, some Java data types are larger than their equivalent C data types. For example, a *char* is 16 bits in Java and (typically) eight bits in C. The numeric data types are similar to those you find on UNIX systems, but they are typically larger than ones on MS-DOS based systems. An *int* is usually two bytes on MS-DOS, for example, but it is four bytes in Java. The sizes for Java data types are the same across all supported platforms, which makes the language more portable.

Listings 1 and 2 show a sample Java program and a sample C function (tested on Windows 95 and Solaris), respectively. The purpose of this sample application is simple. The Java class calls a C function with certain parameters. The C function prints the values in these parameters to *stdout* using *printf* and returns the number of characters printed to the Java class, which in turn prints a message indicating how many characters were printed.

Let's review some of the significant points in these examples. In the Java program, notice how I placed the native method in a separate class (*PrintInC*) from the "main" class (*ThePrinter*). I did this to show you an alternative way of invoking native methods. Also notice the *static* block in the *PrintInC* class. This is a good place to automatically perform tasks when the class is loaded, which in my case happened to be loading a dynamic library:

```
static { System.loadLibrary("print"); }
```

Now, let's consider the C implementation. First notice that I include a StubPreamble.h header file. This is a JDK include file which contains necessary structures (such as *HArrayOfInt*), functions prototypes (such as *makeCString*), and macros (such as *unhand*). Note also the mapping of data types used in Java versus what I had to use in C:

```
public native int doPrint(long l,
    int      i[],
    int      count,
    double d,
    String s);

long PrintInC_doPrint(struct HPrintInC *this,
    int64_t l,
    HArrayOfInt *ai, long iCount,
    double d,
    struct Hjava_lang_String *s)
```

Notice how each *int* has been mapped to *long*. An *int* may be only two bytes on MS-DOS but is always four bytes in Java. Similarly, a Java *long* argument has been mapped to the type *int64_t* in C. The other two notable parameters in these examples are a Java array (*int[]*) and a Java object (*String*). The Java *int[]* array gets mapped to the C structure *HArrayOfInt*.

HArrayOfInt is one example of a standard naming convention used in the *StubPreamble.h* header file. Other examples include *HArrayOfLong*, *HArrayOfByte*, and so on. Java objects also use standard naming conventions such as *H* for handle, the name of the language (e.g. *java*), the package (class library) containing the class (*lang*), and the name of the object (*String*). So a structure for the Java *String* object, which is part of the *lang* package, is named *Hjava_lang_String*.

Finally, let me point out a C macro (*unhand*) and function (*makeCString*) used in this example. The *unhand* macro provides access to the variables in Java's C Structures, such as the *HArrayOfInt*, as shown here:

```
i = unhand(ai)->body;
```

Another example of *unhand* is shown in the next section.

The *makeCString* function takes a Java *String* as an argument and returns a corresponding *char* pointer. There are two other functions related to conversions between Java strings and C character arrays, *makeJavaString* and *java2Cstring*. The former is covered in the next section along with an example. The latter is similar to *makeCString*, except that it works more like *strncpy* — it copies a Java *String* object into an existing *char* array as shown in the following example:

```
char OutFile[127+1];
javaString2CString(pOutFile, OutFile, sizeof(OutFile));
```

Accessing Java Objects

So far I have shown you how to call C functions from Java. Now I show you how to go the other way, accessing Java objects from C. Java provides the ability for C functions to access data members in Java objects, create instances of Java classes, and invoke dynamic and static methods in the Java class. Listings 3 and 4 demonstrate how to accomplish most of these tasks.

Listing 3 contains mostly the same type of Java source code as my previous examples, but one thing is done slightly differently and worth mentioning. The *JavaAccessor* class illustrates how a Java class containing multiple native methods can be instantiated and then individual methods in that class can be invoked, as shown here:

```
JavaAccessor ja = new JavaAccessor();
. .
System.out.println("PATH=" + ja.getEnv("PATH"));
ja.deleteFile("dummy.txt");
```

Listing 4 requires a little more explanation, as there are several new things I have not covered yet. First, the *getEnv* native method returns a Java object (*String*), unlike the other examples I have shown so far which return native data types. Notice how you have to use *makeJavaString*, the opposite of *makeCString*, to return a Java *String* object:

```
return makeJavaString(value, strlen(value));
```

You can access data members from the "automatic" parameter that is passed to every native method, in this case the pointer to *HJavaAccessor*. You simply reference a data member in a Java class by using the *unhand* macro to dereference the Java object:

```
long JavaAccessor_deleteFile(struct HJavaAccessor *javaObj,
    struct Hjava_lang_String *fileName)
{
    ...
    unhand(javaObj)->delRC=rc;
```

Finally, you can instantiate Java classes and invoke methods within them. Three C functions accomplish this — *execute_java_constructor, execute_java_dynamic_method*, and *execute_java_static_method*.

execute_java_constructor (shown below) expects at least four parameters. It can require more, depending on the number of parameters a constructor requires. The first parameter indicates the language/execution environment, which for our purposes is always zero for Java. The second parameter is the name of the Java class. The third is currently reserved for future use. The fourth is the signature of the constructor, and the remaining arguments are any parameters to pass to the constructor.

The signature specified in the fourth parameter is made up of a set of parentheses which contain symbols for a method's parameters. For example, since *JavaAccessor*'s constructor expects no parameters, it simply has the signature *"()"*:

```
hJavaAccessor=(HJavaAccessor *)
    execute_java_constructor(0, "JavaAccessor", 0,"()");
```

Similarly, *execute_java_dynamic_method* (shown below) also expects at least four parameters. It can require more, depending on the number of parameters the Java method requires. The first parameter indicates the language environment, which again is zero for Java. The second parameter is a reference to the Java object created via the *execute_java_constructor* function. The third parameter is the name of the method to invoke. The fourth is the method's signature, and the remaining arguments are any parameters to pass to the method.

As shown in this example, the Java method *"printRC"* expects a single argument of type *int (I)* and does not return any values, so it has a *V* (for void) to indicate this at the right side of the closing parenthesis:

```
if (hJavaAccessor)
    execute_java_dynamic_method(0,
        (HObject *)hJavaAccessor,
        "printRC",
        "(I)V", rc);
```

One good way to find out what letters to use for data types in the signature is to define native methods in a dummy java class and then generate a stub file using the javah utility. You can then inspect the *generated .c file,* which will have comments indicating the signature types. For example, Listing 5 shows a stub file generated from the following Java class:

```
class test
{
    public native long LONG();
    public native float FLOAT();
    public native boolean BOOLEAN();
    public native void MIX_PARMS(
        int i, long l,
        String s, byte b,
        float f, double d,
        char c, boolean bool,
        short si, int[] ai);
}
```

Exceptions and Thread Synchronization

C functions called by Java classes can throw exceptions, which can be caught by Java methods. This is accomplished by the *SignalError* C function provided in the Java library. Consider this line taken from Listing 4:

```
SignalError(0,"java/lang/NullPointerException",0);
```

Java is multi-threaded language, hence C functions used in Java could potentially be accessed concurrently by various threads in a given Java program. Java provides a data-locking mechanism which permits thread-safe operations in Java and native methods. For C functions written for Java, thread-safe operations can be accomplished by using the *synchronized* keyword in the Java method declaration (as shown below) and three C functions provided in the JDK: *monitorWait, monitorNotify,* and *monitorNotifyAll.*

```
public synchronized native String getEnv(String var);
```

Conclusion

Java is a feature-rich language that comes bundled with packages for everything from local file I/O, to socket communications, to GUI programming, to classes for the World Wide Web. Still, there might be times where you need to drop down to C or C++ to accomplish specific tasks, or perhaps to leverage existing C routines or a C API library. For these times, it is nice to know that Java provides the ability to do so. However, one thing to keep in mind is that, whenever possible, any C functions written for Java should be kept as portable and ANSI compliant as possible.

Portability is a big benefit of Java, and it would be nice if you could have the C code be portable as well.

If you do not yet own a book on Java, try downloading the free documentation from Sun Microsystems' FTP site (ftp.javasoft.com). *The Java Tutorial,* by Mary Campione and Kathy Walrath, is an excellent source of information for learning Java. It is available on the Web site in two formats, HTML and PostScript.

Listing 1: Sample Java program

```
// ThePrinter:
// Call native methods to print stuff

public class ThePrinter
{
   public static void main(String args[])
   {
      int count=4;
      int  i[] = new int[count];
      i[0] = 10;
      i[1] = 75;
      i[2] = 95;
      i[3] = 115;

      int printed = new PrintInC().doPrint(25,
                                 i, count,
                                    100.33,
                                 "Hello C");

      System.out.println("Java: " + printed + " chars printed");
   }
}

class PrintInC
{
   public native int doPrint(long    l,
                             int     i[],
                             int     count,
                             double d,
                             String s);

   static
   { System.loadLibrary("print");   }
}
// End of file
```

Listing 2: *PrintInCImp.c*: C functions for Java class

```c
#include <stdio.h>
#include <StubPreamble.h>
#include "PrintInC.h"


/*** Java to C demo: Print data values ***/
long PrintInC_doPrint(struct HPrintInC *this,
                      int64_t l,
                      HArrayOfInt *ai, long iCount,
                      double d,
                      struct Hjava_lang_String *s)
{
   int charsPrinted=0, idx=0;
   long *i;


   /* Print value of "long" (Java int) */
   charsPrinted += printf("C: l = %ld\n", l);


   /* Print array of longs */
   i = unhand(ai)->body;
   for (idx=0; idx < iCount; idx++)
      charsPrinted += printf("C: i[%d] = %d\n", idx, i[idx]);


   /* Print value of "double */
   charsPrinted += printf("C: d = %f\n", d);


   /* Print Java string */
   charsPrinted += printf("C: s = %s\n", makeCString(s));


   /* Return total characters printed */
   return charsPrinted;
}
// End of file
```

Listing 3: Demonstrates Java Object Access

```java
public class JavaAccessor
{
   public synchronized native String getEnv(String var)
         throws java.lang.NullPointerException;

   public native int deleteFile(String fileName);
   public int delRC=0;


   public static void main(String args[])
   {
```

```
          System.loadLibrary("ja");
          JavaAccessor ja = new JavaAccessor();

          try System.out.println("PATH=" +
                    ja.getEnv("PATH"));
          catch(java.lang.NullPointerException e)
          {
            System.out.println("getEnv returned NULL!");
          }

          ja.deleteFile("dummy.txt");
          System.out.println("Return code from"+
                         " deleteFile() = "+
                         ja.delRC);
     }

   public void printRC(int RC)
   {
        System.out.println("Java: RC=" + RC);
   }
}
// End of file
```

Listing 4: Access to Java environment from C

```
#include <stdio.h>
#include <string.h>

#include "JavaAccessor.h"


/*** Get environment variable ***/
struct Hjava_lang_String
    *JavaAccessor_getEnv(
        struct HJavaAccessor *javaObj,
        struct Hjava_lang_String *varName)
{
   char *var=makeCString(varName), *value;

   value=getenv(var);
   if (!value)
   {
       SignalError(0,
                 "java/lang/NullPointerException",
                 0);
       return NULL;
   }

   return makeJavaString(value,strlen(value));
}
```

```
/*** Delete a local file ***/
long JavaAccessor_deleteFile(
        struct HJavaAccessor *javaObj,
        struct Hjava_lang_String *fileName)
{
   HJavaAccessor *hJavaAccessor;
   int rc=unlink(makeCString(fileName));
   unhand(javaObj)->delRC=rc;

   hJavaAccessor=(HJavaAccessor *)
       execute_java_constructor(0,
                    "JavaAccessor",
                            0,
                        "()");

   if (hJavaAccessor)
       execute_java_dynamic_method(0,
           (HObject *)hJavaAccessor,
                       "printRC",
                        "(I)V",
                          rc);
   else
      printf("Unable to create hJavaAccessor\n");

   return rc;
}
```

Listing 5: Stub File generated from Java Class

```
#include <StubPreamble.h>

/* Stubs for class test */
/* SYMBOL: "test/LONG()J", Java_test_LONG_stub */
stack_item *Java_test_LONG_stub(stack_item *_P_,struct execenv *_EE_) {
        Java8 _tval;
        extern int64_t test_LONG(void *);
        SET_INT64(_tval, _P_, test_LONG(_P_[0].p));
        return _P_ + 2;
}
/* SYMBOL: "test/FLOAT()F", Java_test_FLOAT_stub */
stack_item *Java_test_FLOAT_stub(stack_item *_P_,struct execenv *_EE_) {
        extern float test_FLOAT(void *);
        _P_[0].f = test_FLOAT(_P_[0].p);
        return _P_ + 1;
}
/* SYMBOL: "test/BOOLEAN()Z", Java_test_BOOLEAN_stub */
stack_item *Java_test_BOOLEAN_stub(stack_item *_P_,struct execenv *_EE_) {
        extern long test_BOOLEAN(void *);
        _P_[0].i = (test_BOOLEAN(_P_[0].p) ? TRUE : FALSE);
        return _P_ + 1;
}
```

```
/* SYMBOL: "test/MIX_PARMS(IJLjava/lang/String;BFDCZS[I)V",
              Java_test_MIX_0005fP
ARMS_stub */
stack_item *Java_test_MIX_0005fPARMS_stub(stack_item *_P_,struct execenv *_EE_)
{
        Java8 _t2;
        Java8 _t7;
        extern void test_MIX_PARMS(void *,long,int64_t,void *,long,float,double,
long,long,long,void *);
        (void) test_MIX_PARMS(_P_[0].p,((_P_[1].i)),GET_INT64(_t2,
              _P_+2),((_P_[4].p)),((_P_[5].i)),((_P_[6].f)),GET_DOUBLE(_t7,
              _P_+7),((_P_[9].i)),((_P_[10].i)),((_P_[11].i)),((_P_[12].p)));
        return _P_;
}

/* End of file */
```

End Listings

Calling Native Code from Java

Robi Khan

One of the benefits of programming in Java is that the Java Virtual Machine (VM) hides platform differences. Applications can be developed once and run anywhere a Java VM is implemented. Unfortunately, that abstraction can get in the way of developing full-featured applications. Although the AWT user-interface package, for instance, provides a reasonable way to write cross-platform GUI code, it lacks some basic services that users take for granted. For example, AWT doesn't offer clipboard support. So even though all major GUIs (Windows, Mac, Motif) have a clipboard, there's no way to access it from Java. While it's relatively trivial to code a Java clipboard, it would be nicer if the real clipboard were available, so data could be exchanged with other applications.

In this article I'll use native code to implement a Java *Clipboard* class that does just that. Though the implementation of the *Clipboard* class is for Win32, the basic principles of calling native code are the same on all Java platforms.

The tools and documentation needed to write native methods are provided in the Java Development Kit (JDK) (http:// www.javasoft.com). I used JDK 1.0.2 and Visual C++ 2.2 (4.x should work just as well) in implementing *Clipboard.* The complete source code and related files are available electronically on the CD-ROM.

Robi is a developer at Corel Corp., where he works on Java-related software projects. He can be reached at robik@corel.com. Reprinted courtesy of Dr. Dobb's Sourcebook.

Purists may question using native code, since it is nonportable. Java applets (as opposed to applications) aren't even allowed to load native libraries for security reasons. Still, certain projects demand access to native code. Anyone porting Java to a new platform must use the native-code interface to call the underlying operating system APIs. People writing stand-alone Java applications often need to use existing code libraries until Java versions become available. In some cases, execution speed may be critical enough that only compiled C/C++ code will suffice.

Declaring Native Methods

Java doesn't support functions that exist outside a class—all functions are methods bound to some Java object. So how can Java programs call native C code, where objects and methods don't exist?

The answer is that native code must be wrapped up in a Java class definition. A Java class can be created where the methods are declared in the standard fashion, but implemented in a C (or C++) library. These methods are called "native" methods, and are identified by the *native* modifier.

A native method is just like a normal Java method except the implementation is absent. As Listing One illustrates, the *Clipboard* class has four native methods. Notice that the class has a static block of code; this is how the library containing the native code is loaded. This library is a DLL on Win32, a shared library on the Macintosh, and shared object (.so) under Solaris.

```
(a)   javac Clipboard

(b)   javah Clipboard

(c)   javah java.io.InputStream
      javah java.lang.String
```

Example 1: *(a) Compiling a class with native methods; (b) javah reads a .class file and outputs a header; (c) generating class definitions.*

Defining and Implementing the Class

Once a class with native methods is defined, it's compiled like any other Java file (I used the JDK 1.0.2 javac compiler) to produce a .class file; see Example 1(a).

```
(a)   extern void Clipboard_clear(struct HClipboard *hclip);

(b)   extern void Clipboard_clear(struct HClipboard *this_ptr)
      {
          ...
          if( unhand(this_ptr)->auto_empty ) ...
```

Example 2: *(a) Functions all have the same first parameter; (b) the* Clipboard_getText *function uses unhand to check the* auto_empty *member variable.*

To allow access to the *Clipboard* object definition from native code, a header file and stubs file are needed. The JDK tool javah does this. It reads a .class file and outputs a header with the equivalent C definition; see Example 1(b). (Note that javah takes a class name—not a filename—as its argument. This means that any class javah can find, including the standard java classes or those specified in the CLASSPATH, can be used as an argument.) You can easily generate class definitions for any class in the CLASSPATH; see Example 1(c).

The generated header file, Clipboard.h, shows what the class looks like to C programs; see Listing Two.

The *ClassClipboard* struct mirrors the definition of the *Clipboard* class. The lone member variable in the class, the Boolean *auto_empty,* is defined in the C version as a *long.*

Javah generates a function prototype for each native method. The function names are derived from the class name and method name; the string *Clipboard_* is prepended to the method names to form the function names. If *Clipboard* were defined as part of a package (say, *my.ui.Clipboard)* the function names would begin with *my_ui_Clipboard_* instead.

Javah also does the work of generating the stubs file. The stubs file is a C file that implements some glue code for the Java VM. Invoking a native method at run time will cause the VM to call a stub function, which, in turn, will call the function implementation. The stubs are generated using the *–stubs* option, passing the same class name used when generating the header. In this case, the stubs file will be Clipboard.c *(javah –stubs Clipboard).*

The actual implementation of *Clipboard,* ClipboardImpl.cpp, is written in C++. Using C++ for the implementation is just as easy as using C. The only requirement is that the class header be surrounded in an *extern "C"* wrapper. The implementation file implements the functions prototyped in Clipboard.h, calling various Win32 APIs to manipulate the clipboard; see Listing Three.

```
Method:    boolean startsWith(String prefix, int toffset);
Signature:   "(Ljava/lang/String;I)Z"

Method:    void run();
Signature:   "()V"

Method:    Object put(Object key, Object value)
Signature:   "(Ljava/lang/Object;Ljava/lang/Object;)Ljava/lang/Object;"

Method:    void writeChars(char char_array[])
Signature:   "([C)V;"
```

Figure 1: *Method declarations and equivalent signatures.*

Building the DLL

The final step in the native implementation is creating a DLL from the header, stub, and implementation files. The DLL I'll create here is Clipboard.dll.

No special work has to be done to export functions in the DLL—the stubs file already exports the required entry points. To build the library, the stubs and implementation files (Clipboard.c and Clipboard.cpp) should be compiled and linked into the same DLL. The Java VM import library (javai.lib, found in the JDK lib directory) should also be linked in: It provides entry points that allow the native code to instantiate and call Java objects.

The *Clipboard* class explicitly loads the Clipboard DLL in a piece of static code run at class-load time. Once the DLL is loaded, calls to any of the native methods are resolved dynamically by the VM using *GetProcAddress()*. You should be aware that if a native method is missing from the DLL, no error will occur until Java tries to call it (at which point it will throw a *LinkageError* exception). Similarly, if the entire DLL is missing or cannot be found, Java will throw an *UnsatisfiedLinkError* when *System.load* is called.

The sample code includes an external makefile for Visual C++. Just run nmake and all the necessary files will be built. The makefile requires that

- The JDK 1.0.2 is properly installed.

- The ALT_BOOTDIR environment variable is set to the JDK installation directory.

- The JDK tools are in the PATH.

```
(a)   HObject *execute_java_constructor(struct execenv *ee,
           char *classname, ClassClass *c, char *signature, ... );
      long execute_java_dynamic_method(struct execenv *ee,
         HObject *obj, char *method_name, char *signature, ... );
      long execute_java_static_method(struct execenv *ee,
         ClassClass *c,  char *method_name, char *signature, ...
      );
      ClassClass *FindClass(struct execenv *, char *classname,
         bool_t resolve);

(b)   ClassClass *      class_info;
      Hjava_lang_string  *string_obj;

      class_info= FindClass( 0, "java/lang/String", true );
      string_obj = (Hjava_lang_string)execute_java_constructor(
      0, 0,class_info, "()" );
```

Example 3: (a) Calling Java objects from C; (b) class info can be loaded using FindClass.

```
(a)   char     a_byte;
             a_byte = (char)execute_java_dynamic_method(0, obj_handle,
                        "someMethodReturningByte", "()B" )

(b)   Hjava_lang_String *clip_string;
             long              retval;
             retval = execute_java_dynamic_method(0, (Hobject
             *)this_ptr,
                                "getText", ()Ljava/lang/String;");
             clip_string = (Hjava_lang_String)retval;
```

Example 4: *(a) Casting the return value; (b) casting the return value to an object handle of the appropriate type.*

The virtual-machine headers that *Clipboard* uses are all part of the JDK's include directory.

Running and Debugging the *Clipboard* Demo

Once everything is built, you can run the demo Java application with the Java interpreter by typing *java NativeDemo.*

NativeDemo uses *Clipboard* to read the contents of the clipboard and prints the text to *System.out.* Then it calls methods to set and retrieve text from the clipboard.

Clipboard's native code can be debugged by running java.exe in the Visual C++ debugger. Just remember to specify *NativeDemo* as the program argument. Also, add Clipboard.dll to the list of additional DLLs in the debug-settings property page.

Java Object Handles

If you look at the function prototypes that javah generates for the *Clipboard* class, you'll notice that all the functions have the same first parameter; see Example 2(a). This parameter is a handle to the object on which the method operates. It is similar to the C++ *this* pointer, except that it is explicitly declared. Like the *this* pointer, the handle provides access to the class-member data.

Unlike C++ object pointers, Java object handles cannot be dereferenced with the -> or * operators. Instead, you must use the *unhand()* macro. This will return a pointer to the object's data. The *Clipboard_getText* function uses *unhand()* to check the *auto_empty* member variable; see Example 2(b).

It may seem tedious to use the *unhand()* macro to dereference object handles every time member data needs to be accessed, but it is necessary. If you dereference the handle and store the data pointer in a temporary variable, you run the risk of the VM moving the data somewhere else when garbage

```
(a)    SignalError( ExecEnv *, char * exception_classname, char * message);

(b)    execute_java_dynamic_method(...)
                If( exceptionOccured( EE() ) ) {
                // some exception happened, so 'catch' it
                   exceptionClear(EE());
                   // will stop unwinding of stack
                }
```

Example 5: *(a) Throwing Java exceptions from native code; (b) catching Java exceptions.*

collection occurs. The VM will prevent garbage collection if your data pointer is declared on the stack, but this feature fails if you store the data pointer in a global. It is just safer to use *unhand()* all the time.

In the same header, you'll notice that javah created a type *HClipboard* as a handle to *Clipboard* objects—it just used the class name to make the type name. For classes that are in packages, javah generates a handle name using the full package and class name. For example, the class *java.lang.String* is referred to internally with a handle named *Hjava_ lang_String*. As another example, *java.io.InputStream* is referred to with *Hjava_io_InputStream*.

Calling Java Code from C

The *Clipboard* class not only calls native code, but uses Java objects like *Strings* and *InputStreams*. Calling Java objects from C is done with a set of functions exported from javai.dll, the virtual machine DLL; see Example 3(a).

The use of these functions is similar; they all take an execution environment as their first parameter. An execution environment stores the state of the Java stack—a zero is usually substituted for this argument to refer to the current environment.

The function *execute_java_constructor* instantiates a Java object, either by class name or by using previously loaded class information (pointed to by a *ClassClass* *). Using preloaded class information is faster than resolving the

```
SomeClass_someMethod( HSomeClass * this_ptr )
{
    monitorWait( obj_monitor(this_ptr), timeout );
    monitorNotify( obj_monitor(this_ptr) );
    monitorNotifyAll( obj_monitor(this_ptr) );
}
```

Example 6: *Converting an object handle into a monitor.*

class by name. Class information can be loaded using *FindClass*; see Example 3(b). When referring to a class by name, use the fully qualified class name, and replace the periods with forward slashes; for example, the class "java.lang.String" is referenced as "java/lang/String."

The *execute_java_static_method* function calls a static method on a class. It requires the class information be found via *FindClass* first. The method to be called is specified by the method name.

Similarly, *execute_java_dynamic_ method* calls a nonstatic method on an object. Instead of class info, you provide a handle to the object on which the method operates. Curiously, the VM does not provide a *FindMethod* call to bind to static or dynamic methods—you always have to specify the method name when calling it.

Method Signatures

When calling a constructor or method, you have to supply a method signature. This is a string that describes the parameters for the method. (The calls take a variable number of parameter arguments.) It resembles *printf* format strings.

The method signature is a string of the form *(<param_type>...)* *<return_type>*. Parameter types are simple, one-character values for intrinsic data types or a class name for objects. If you supply an invalid method signature, an *IncompatibleClassChangeError* exception will be thrown at run time. You should carefully examine method signatures and their parameters, since the parameters are untyped as with *printf*—an incorrect format string could cause a crash.

If you look at the stubs file generated in the example Clipboard.c, you'll see that javah inserts comments with the method signature for each of the native methods. If you are ever unsure about how to code signatures, you can always use *javah –stubs* to generate them directly from a method declaration. You can

Java Type	C Equivalent	Signature
long	int64_t (64-bit integer)	J
integer	long	I
byte	char	B
char	char	C
enum	long	E
float	float	F
double	double	D
boolean	long	Z
void	void	V
JavaObject	HObject * or derived	L<classname>;
Array of <type>	HarrayOf<type> * or HarrayOfObject *	[<type>

Table 1: *How intrinsic Java data types correspond to C data types.*

also use the stubs file to see how intrinsic Java data types correspond to C data types; see Table 1. Figure 1 provides some example method declarations and equivalent signatures.

Method Return Values

Both *execute_java_static_method* and *execute_java_dynamic_method* return a *long*. If the method being called returns an intrinsic type (whose size is less than or equal to a *long*), you can simply cast the return value to that type; see Example 4(a).

For methods that return objects, you can cast the return value to an object handle of the appropriate type, as in ClipboardImpl.cpp; see Example 4(b).

Working with Strings

The VM provides a number of useful routines to convert strings from Java to C and back. The routines are well documented in javastring.h in the JDK include directory.

Catching and Throwing Exceptions

You can throw Java exceptions from native code using the *SignalError* function; see Example 5(a). It will instantiate an *Exception* (or *Exception*-derived) object, and pass a message string to *Exception*'s constructor. Note that *SignalError* will not cause a C *longjmp* or C++ exception—the code will still have to use *return, goto,* or C++ *exception* to exit out of the function. ClipboardImpl.cpp uses a utility function *ThrowClipboardException* that, in turn, calls *SignalError*.

Catching Java exceptions is a little trickier. After looking through the JDK header files, I turned up two macros in interpreter.h, *exceptionOccurred* and *exceptionClear,* that allow you to detect an exception and catch it. First use *exceptionOccurred* to test if any exception has occurred. Then use *exceptionClear* to clear the exception state so that it does not continue unwinding the stack. These macros require an execution environment, and do not accept zero as a default. A valid pointer to the current environment can be obtained via the EE() function; see Example 5(b).

Unfortunately, these macros are not mentioned in the JDK online documentation, so they may not be safe to call. Their use is also limited by the fact that you cannot detect the type of exception that occurred.

Synchronization

If native methods are declared as *synchronized*, no additional work is needed to make them thread safe. The VM will properly synchronize native method calls.

Functions corresponding to the *wait, notify,* and *notifyAll* methods are exported from the VM. The macro *obj_monitor* converts an object handle into a monitor usable by these functions; see Example 6.

Other Native Code Solutions

Both Microsoft and Netscape have alternative methods of accessing native code from Java. Microsoft (which owns the reference implementation of Java on Win32) has created a virtual machine where the run-time layout of Java objects matches that of COM (Component Object Model) objects. This makes Java objects callable as COM objects from C/C++ code, and allows COM objects to be called from Java code. This simplifies the calling protocol between Java and C greatly, and may provide some execution-speed advantages. (Details can be found on Microsoft's web site.) The big disadvantage is that it only works with Microsoft's Java VM, and only on Windows. The original native code interface at least provides source compatibility among platforms. (Microsoft supports the existing interface as well.)

Netscape has recently proposed an enhanced version of the native code interface called JRI, (Java Runtime Interface). It is the same core set of functions, plus additional functionality, including exception handling. Its primary benefit over the Microsoft approach is that it is a platform-independent API. It remains to be seen whether JavaSoft will adopt JRI as a standard Java API.

For most developers, the native method interface, with all its quirks, is the only solution for applications today.

Listing One

```
import java.io.*;

public class Clipboard
{
    static
    {
    try {
        System.loadLibrary("Clipboard");
    } catch(UnsatisfiedLinkError e) {
        System.err.println("Could not load Clipboard dll");
    }
    }
    public Clipboard(boolean auto_empty) {
    this.auto_empty = auto_empty;
    }
    public native void clear();
    public native void putText( String clip_text );
    public native String getText();
    public native InputStream getStream();

    boolean auto_empty;
}
```

Listing Two

```
/* DO NOT EDIT THIS FILE - it is machine generated */
#include <native.h>
/* Header for class Clipboard */

#ifndef _Included_Clipboard
#define _Included_Clipboard

typedef struct ClassClipboard {
    /*boolean*/ long auto_empty;
} ClassClipboard;
HandleTo(Clipboard);

#ifdef __cplusplus
extern "C" {
#endif
extern void Clipboard_clear(struct HClipboard *);
struct Hjava_lang_String;
extern void Clipboard_putText(struct HClipboard *,struct Hjava_lang_String *);
extern struct Hjava_lang_String *Clipboard_getText(struct HClipboard *);
struct Hjava_io_InputStream;
extern struct Hjava_io_InputStream *Clipboard_getStream(struct HClipboard *);
#ifdef __cplusplus
}
#endif
#endif
```

Listing Three

```
// JDK headers do not include #ifdef __cpluscplus/extern "C" guards
// so we surround headers with extern "C"
extern "C" {
#include "Clipboard.h"
#include "java_io_InputStream.h"
#include "java_io_StringBufferInputStream.h"
}
#include "windows.h"

static void ThrowClipboardException(char * message)
{
    // throws a Java exception of type java.lang.Exception
    // and passes a given message string to the exception class constructor
    SignalError(0, "java/lang/Exception", message );
}

// empties the Clipboard
void Clipboard_clear(struct HClipboard *)
{
    BOOL    emptied;

    emptied = EmptyClipboard();
}
// puts the given text string on the clipboard
```

```
void Clipboard_putText(
    struct HClipboard *      this_ptr,
    struct Hjava_lang_String * text_string )
{
    HANDLE  hglb_clip_text;
    char *  text;
    int     text_len;

    if( !OpenClipboard(NULL) || !EmptyClipboard() ) {
    ThrowClipboardException("opening" );
    return;
    }

    // make a C string out of the Java String
    text = makeCString( text_string );
    text_len = lstrlen(text);

    // allocate a global memory object for the text
    hglb_clip_text = GlobalAlloc( GMEM_DDESHARE, text_len + 1 );
    if( hglb_clip_text == NULL ) {
    // couldn't allocate block, so throw a Java exception
    ThrowClipboardException("allocating");
   return;
    }

    LPSTR   lpszClipBuffer;
    // lock the clip buffer, and copy the string into it
    lpszClipBuffer = (LPSTR)GlobalLock(hglb_clip_text);
    if( lpszClipBuffer == NULL ) {
    // couldn't lock memory so throw Java exception
    ThrowClipboardException("locking");
    }
    lstrcpy( lpszClipBuffer, text );
    GlobalUnlock( hglb_clip_text );

    SetClipboardData(CF_TEXT, hglb_clip_text );
    CloseClipboard();
}
// returns the clipboard text as a string
struct Hjava_lang_String *Clipboard_getText(
    struct HClipboard *     this_ptr)
{
    HANDLE  hglb_clip_text;
    char *  text;
    int     text_len;

    if( !OpenClipboard(NULL) ) {
    ThrowClipboardException("opening" );
    return NULL;
    }

    // get the clipboard data
    hglb_clip_text = GetClipboardData(CF_TEXT);
    if( hglb_clip_text == NULL ) {
```

```
    return NULL;
    }

LPSTR        lpszClipBuffer;
Hjava_lang_String * clip_string;

lpszClipBuffer = (LPSTR)GlobalLock(hglb_clip_text);
if( lpszClipBuffer == NULL ) {
ThrowClipboardException("locking");
return NULL;
}
clip_string = makeJavaString(lpszClipBuffer, lstrlen(lpszClipBuffer));

GlobalUnlock( hglb_clip_text);

// if the auto_empty flag is set clear the clipboard
if( unhand(this_ptr)->auto_empty ) {
EmptyClipboard();
}
CloseClipboard();

    return clip_string;
}
// returns the clipboard text data in a stream
struct Hjava_io_InputStream *Clipboard_getStream(
    struct HClipboard * this_ptr )
{
    Hjava_io_StringBufferInputStream *  input_stream;
    long                retval;
    Hjava_lang_String *         clip_string;

    // call Clipboard.getString to get clipboard text
    retval = execute_java_dynamic_method( 0, (HObject *)this_ptr, "getText",
    "()Ljava/lang/String;" );
    clip_string = (Hjava_lang_String *)retval;
    // construct a StringBufferInputStream from the string
    input_stream =(Hjava_io_StringBufferInputStream *)execute_java_constructor(
        0, "java/io/StringBufferInputStream", 0, "(Ljava/lang/String;)",
        clip_string );
    // StringBufferInputStream is derived from InputStream,
    // so this cast is perfectly valid
    return (Hjava_io_InputStream *)input_stream;
}
```

End Listings

Automatically Generating Java Documentation

Gary Aitken

In my article "Moving from C++ to Java," I pointed out that everything about a Java class is contained in a single file—there are no separate header files as in C and C++. Since the code to implement a method must appear with the method definition, it is difficult to look at any Java source and get an impression of how a class should be used. If you have a binary Java class library, there is no associated source code to look at. The information conveyed by a traditional C/C++ header file is encoded in the compiled Java binary, and although the compiler can find it, that doesn't do you much good. Since you can no longer get a concise summary of the interface to a class, you have to scan the entire source file to find each little piece. Consequently, documentation is of paramount importance in the Java environment. In this article, I'll examine some of the documentation issues related to Java programming and discuss how to automatically generate documentation for Java classes.

Gary has been technical lead and chief architect for a large commercial UNIX-based C++ toolkit for the past seven years. Reprinted courtesy of Dr. Dobb's Journal.

You can think of code as many different things:

- An executable program that performs some function.
- A collection of classes that are used in concert to implement a program.
- A collection of methods that implement the functionality provided by a particular class, or that define the functionality of an interface.
- Individual lines of code that implement a particular algorithm or functional capability within a single method.

Based on these categories, how you think of code determines what your documentation will explain:

- How to use the application.
- Which classes are exported (made publicly available), and their general purposes.
- How to use the individual methods for each class.
- How the algorithms that implement each method work.

Java introduces an additional kind of comment, known as a "doc comment," to help automate the process of producing programmer documentation and to ensure that the documentation matches the actual code. The standard Java environment includes a tool named "javadoc" that processes Java source files and produces a set of HTML documentation files—Web pages—from the doc comments. The doc comment, in combination with javadoc, addresses the documentation issues involved in exporting classes and using methods for each class. If you provide the proper comments in the code, at least some of the documentation can be produced automatically, in a form suitable for online use. While not required by the Java environment, if you are going to produce classes that others can easily reuse, you should start getting into the habit of including appropriate doc comments in every Java class you write. You should also keep the documentation up to date whenever you change the signature of a method.

Javadoc produces HTML documentation in a particular format. Other processors will probably appear that produce output in different forms, all from the same embedded doc comments. (In fact, javadoc currently can also produce FrameMaker .MIF format, an undocumented capability.)

For each public class or interface (.java file), javadoc produces HTML pages with the following components, in the order listed:

1. Header.
2. Class hierarchy diagram.
3. Class description.

4. Index of public data fields, sorted alphabetically, with static and instance variables intermixed.

5. Index of constructors.

6. Index of public methods, sorted alphabetically, with static and normal methods intermixed.

7. Description of public variables, in the order they appear in the source file.

8. Description of public constructors, in the order they appear in the source file.

9. Description of public methods, in the order they appear in the source file.

Javadoc will include an entry for all public classes, variables, and methods, whether or not they have a doc comment associated with them. The descriptions—public variables, constructors, and methods—appear in the same order in which the items appear in the source file (on the assumption that you have tried to group related functions together).

Machine-generated documentation is going to become commonplace as a result of programs like javadoc. This documentation is a reflection of the quality of your professional work, and since no one is going to edit the automatically produced documentation, it behooves you to include the best possible doc comments you can. Besides, it makes good sense—adequate documentation means coworkers won't waste time deciphering code they aren't particularly interested in, simply to learn how to use it.

```
(a)   /**
       * Summary Line
       * Zero or more lines of detail text; may
           include HTML and multiple paragraphs
       * @xxx  zero or more tag lines, as appropriate
       */

(b)   /**
      Summary line
      Zero or more lines of detail text; may include
        HTML and multiple paragraphs
      @xxx  zero or more tag lines, as appropriate
      */
```

Figure 1: *Two proper format styles for doc comments.*

Doc Comment Syntax

The doc comment uses the form /** ... */. Whether the comment is used by javadoc to produce documentation is context sensitive. Doc comments are only significant to javadoc in the following circumstances:

- Immediately before a class definition.
- Immediately before a public member function.
- Immediately before a public data member.

A single doc comment should be used for each situation; if multiple doc comments are encountered preceding a particular definition, only the last one is used.

Within any particular line of a doc comment, leading space and a sequence of one or more consecutive asterisk characters are ignored.

Depending on the context, a doc comment may contain additional keywords, or tags, that flag components to be specially treated. All tags start with @. To be recognized, tags are supposed to be at the beginning of the line on which they appear. Any leading spaces followed by asterisks are ignored, so the sequence * *@sometag* is recognized as a tag. Note that horizontal tab characters are *not* allowed in this leading sequence.

Table 1 lists the special tags and the circumstances in which they may appear. Lines containing unknown tags are included as normal text in the preceding item; case is important.

Each doc comment is composed of the following:

Summary line. The first "nonempty" line of a doc comment has particular significance. It is used as a summary, and is inserted as a one-line synopsis in the appropriate index (components 4–6 of the generated HTML). "Nonempty," in this case, means a line containing nonwhitespace other than "/**"

	Tag	Example
(a)	@see class-name	@see MyClass
	@see class-name#method	@see MyClass#func1
	@see fully-qualified-class-name	@see MyPkg.MyClass
	@see fully-qualified-class-name#method	@see MyPkg.MyClass#func1
	@version arbitrary-text	@version 1.0
	@author arbitrary-text	@author Your Name
(b)	@see (any of the above forms)	
(c)	@see (any of the above forms)	
	@return arbitrary-text	@return Number of gophers
	@param parameter-name arbitrary-text	@param n Number of items needed
	@exception exception-class-name arbitrary-text	@exception MyException When something happens...

Table 1: *Doc comment tags: (a) class-definition tags; (b) variable-definition tags; (c) method-definition tags.*

(the first line of the doc comment, which may also contain text) or a series of spaces followed by a series of one or more asterisks.

Normal text lines. Lines containing normal text follow the summary line. These lines are considered part of the detailed textual explanation. They are treated as HTML, so line breaks, tabs, and extra spaces do not normally have any significance. They may contain normal HTML tags, which allow special formatting for things like code examples. They should not, however, include HTML tags used for header information, since javadoc inserts its own header information throughout the document.

Tagged lines. These lines should always appear after the detail lines. Lines containing tags are not sorted by tag, so you should keep all tags of the same type together—all *@param* lines together, all *@exception* lines together, and so on. The arbitrary-text portion of a tagged line may extend over multiple lines. Any lines following the last tagged line will contain the formatting style of the last tagged line and will appear to be part of the documentation for the last tagged line. What this means, for practical purposes, is that your doc comments should look like Figure 1(a) or 1(b), and order *is* important.

Generating HTML

The documentation available for the javadoc tool is somewhat sparse. Javadoc is invoked by entering *javadoc [options] packageName1 packageName2. . . classPath1.java classPath2.java. . . .* Allowable options are as follows:

- *-authors.* An undocumented option required to generate the author entry from *@author* tags. The option flag is plural ("authors") but the corresponding doc comment tag is singular (*@author*).

- *-version.* An undocumented option required to generate the version entry from an *@version* tag.

- *-noindex.* An undocumented option that prevents the AllNames.html file from being generated.

- *-notree.* An undocumented option that prevents the tree.html file from being generated.

- *-doctype {MIF | HTML}.* An undocumented option that determines the type of document generated. The default is HTML, but specifying *-doctype MIF* will cause FrameMaker .MIF files to be generated.

- *-classpath path.* Specifies the class search path to be used. Assuming you can compile your source from the directory in which you invoke javadoc, this flag should not be necessary.

- *-d docdir.* Specifies where to put the results. While this is an optional argument, it is mandatory to get correct output and has only one possible correct value, unless you are going to move the generated documentation to its final destination prior to use.

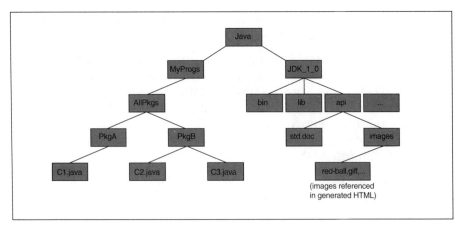

Figure 2: *Sample directory structure.*

Javadoc generates output with relative pathnames for the hypertext links. In theory, this means the destination documentation directory could be anywhere. However, because all of your Java classes will have links to the base Java language documentation, and these links also are relative, the destination directory must be the same as the directory that contains the API docs for the standard Java distribution.

If you invoke javadoc and specify path names to classes, the generated HTML files will contain correct pages for the individual classes, but any index and package pages will be incomplete. For this reason, I suggest you always generate the documentation for a complete system using the package arguments instead of individual .java class paths. Note the differences in the way the two types of arguments are entered—individual classes are specified using a normal file name (for example, *AllPkgs\PkgA\MyClass.java*) while packages are specified using package names, such as *AllPkgs.PkgA*.

To illustrate, assume you have a directory structure like Figure 2. Your Java code is in two packages, AllPkgs.PkgA and AllPkgs.PkgB. The JDK 1.0 distribution is under JDK_1_0, with the API documentation in the API subdirectory. If you position at java\MyProgs (UNIX users switch all occurrences of \ in pathnames to /), you would generate the complete documentation for all of your packages by invoking javadoc as: javadoc -version -authors -d java\JDK_1_0\api AllPkgs.PkgA AllPkgs.PkgB. This would produce the files in Figure 3. Unfortunately, you can't just point javadoc at the top-level directory (AllPkgs); it does not recurse.

The generated HTML will contain references to images in a subdirectory named "images." The images already exist in the "images" subdirectory for the standard Java API documentation from the distribution. If you install the HTML in the same directory as the standard Java distribution, everything will work fine. Otherwise, you will need to either copy the subdirectory containing the images to the directory where you install your documentation, or make a symbolic link to the images subdirectory (UNIX users). Note again, however, that if you do not install in the same directory as the Java API documentation, the links from your documentation to base language pages will be incorrect.

Make sure all classes compile properly before attempting to generate any documentation. Javadoc spits out all sorts of errors when working with incorrect code.

The *@see* tag produces references to the indicated classes and functions. Unfortunately, if the reference is to a class or method that is not part of the class in which the *@see* occurs, Javadoc produces HTML that displays only the final class or method name instead of the fully qualified name. You may become confused if there are similarly named methods in different classes. The reference is correct, and one can decipher it by examining the tag if the HTML browser displays it, but it is not obvious when reading the text.

The *@version* and *@author* tags cause entries to appear in the generated HTML files only if the undocumented command line options *-version* and *-authors* are used.

If you use some form of source control, you will probably want to include the source control information on the *@version* line.

Some (Hopefully Productive) Design Criticism

Unfortunately, doc comments are only relevant immediately preceding a class, variable, or method definition; and the javadoc tool only deals with these comments. It is well known that documentation removed from the immediate source line to which it applies is more prone to error than documentation directly associated with the code. When the source line changes, the related comment line is frequently overlooked. It would have been much better if the doc comment had been allowed in the source line of interest, as well as before it. Consider the method definition and associated doc comment in Figure 4.

During the development cycle, arguments, return values, and method names change. This virtually guarantees that some of the documentation will be wrong because it is not located on the same physical line as the quantity to

```
java\JDK_1_0\api\AllPkgs.PkgA.C1.html      AllPkgs.PkgA.C1 doc
java\JDK_1_0\api\AllPkgs.PkgB.C2.html      AllPkgs.PkgB.C2 doc
java\JDK_1_0\api\AllPkgs.PkgB.C3.html      AllPkgs.PkgB.C3 doc
java\JDK_1_0\api\AllNames.html             Index of all classes, methods,
                                              and variables
java\JDK_1_0\api\tree.html                 Class hierarchy
java\JDK_1_0\api\packages.html             Index to all packages
java\JDK_1_0\api\Package-AllPkgs.PkgA.html Index to individual class doc
                                              in PkgA
java\JDK_1_0\api\Package-AllPkgs.PkgB.html Index to individual class doc
                                              in PkgB
```

Figure 3: *Typical output files.*

which it refers. The number of incorrect comments will increase over time in most situations. With the current doc comments, there is no guarantee that the parameter name listed in the doc comment matches the name used in the function prototype. "Out of sight, out of mind" applies to these situations, and the doc comment will rapidly be scrolled off the page as the programmer concentrates on the task at hand—the code below the definition.

If doc comments were allowed in the definition itself, this problem could be avoided. As Figure 5 shows, the doc comment for each quantity of interest is on the same line as the item of interest; as a result, a programmer is much more likely to see it and update it. The hypothetical *@method* tag could be automatically replaced by the method name. Perhaps a future revision will allow this. It requires slightly more intelligent parsing of the source, but certainly nothing particularly difficult, and it would increase the reliability of the automatically generated documentation. An obvious enhancement would be to allow //* to introduce a single-line doc comment.

Other Problems with Doc Comments

A related problem comes from the current lack of good supporting development editors. The most likely source for the original text of a doc comment is an existing doc comment. Perhaps 99 percent of all comments of this type are generated by cutting and pasting the text from an existing method and then editing it. Unfortunately, there are too many situations where the text gets cut and pasted, but not edited. Smart editors could automatically insert appropriate doc comments when a new public function is introduced and could make sure each element is at least modified (or flagged) before the file is saved. They could also force a check when the type of a parameter, exception, or return value is modified or a new one is added.

```
/**
 * Locate a complete user description by user name.
 * @return      Complete description of a user.
 * @param       last                Last name, arbitrary text
 * @param       first               First name, arbitrary text
 * @param       middle              Middle name(s), arbitrary text
 * @exception NoUserException       User is not in the database
 */
public User findUser( String last, String first, String middle )
    throws NoUserException
{
    code to implement method
}
```

Figure 4: *Typical doc comment and associated method definition.*

Nonpublic Classes in a Source File

While a Java source file is limited to containing only one public class definition, it may contain many private class definitions that are not exported. These private class definitions may also contain doc comments. When javadoc is invoked and passed the name of a Java source file, it creates a separate HTML documentation file for each class defined in the source file, regardless of whether the classes are public or private. When invoked with a package name, javadoc does not generate the HTML files for private classes.

Javap: A Last Resort and Sanity Check

What happens if you get a binary distribution of a set of Java classes and the documentation doesn't match the binary? Or if there is no documentation at all? The standard Java distribution includes a disassembler called "javap" to address these problems. When invoked with the name of a class, javap searches the CLASSPATH for a corresponding compiled class definition and prints out the class definition showing a partial signature of all public methods and all fields. Unfortunately, this is seldom useful, since the formal parameter names are missing, and only their types remain. You can find out the method names and their parameter and return value types, but you have no argument names to give you any hint of what the parameters mean. The exceptions are not listed either, although this is not a big problem because the compiler will tell you if you forget about one of them.

It would have been useful if the compiled class file contained the doc comments as well as the code; then the binary version of a class could be a truly self-contained unit. Doing so would have significantly increased the size of a binary file, with corresponding increases in the time required to download a class over the Net; though it would be easy to strip out doc comments on a

```
/**
 * @method attempts to locate a user in the global user database.
 */
public User   /** Complete description of a user. */
  findUser(   /** Locate a complete user description by user name */
  String  last,   /** Last name, arbitrary text */
  String  first,  /** First name, arbitrary text */
  String  middle) /** Middle name(s), arbitrary text */
  throws  NoUserException /** User is not in the database */
{
  code to implement method
}
```

Figure 5: *Placing the doc comment for each quantity of interest on the same line as the item of interest would encourage comment updating.*

download for the purposes of execution. It would have made sense to allow inclusion of doc-comment information at least as an option to the compiler.

A Complete Documentation Set

By taking a little care and using appropriate doc comments instead of normal comments in your Java source code, you can get two jobs done at once—documenting your code for future reference by yourself and your coworkers and producing real, usable online documentation for other users of your classes through the use of javadoc.

Acknowledgment

Many thanks to Peter Parnes for his help deciphering some of the undocumented options for javadoc.

Leveraging Your Visual C++ Experience

David C. Mitchell

There you are, minding your own business, trying to get some real work done, while the rest of the world surfs the Net. You've got nothing against HTML or Web pages, and both Java and ActiveX look promising. But you've been so busy building giant programs using Visual C++, you just haven't had time to sort through all the hype and figure out exactly which tools you're going to use to take these real applications to the Internet.

Let's discuss what you as a developer can do to exploit your Visual C++ experience in the Internet environment. I'll present a way to use the Internet deployment standards offered by Java and still maintain C++ development (including the C++ code that you are currently working on). I'll also focus on the thin client model and why it is best suited for Internet applications. You'll see why traditional client/server models have limited flexibility in the context

David is the founder and chief technical officer of ViewSoft, a provider of thin client Internet development technology. He can be reached at davem@viewsoft.com or www.viewsoft.com. Reprinted courtesy of Microsoft Systems Journal.

of the Internet. I'll develop a "litmus test" for determining how effective an application's architecture is at exploiting the Internet. Based on the litmus test, I'll define a framework that allows you to create thin client applications and deploy them over the Internet using Java's cross-platform toolkit, AWT. I'll include various code examples that demonstrate a framework that has already been developed.

A pared-down version of this framework along with support tools to use the framework is available on http://www.msj.com or on the CD-ROM. The framework and tools supplied are sufficient to develop all of the samples in this article. For this article, I'll focus on the Java solution—in a future article, I'll show you how to use ActiveX to develop a thin client.

What's Interesting About the Internet?

Before jumping in on the thin client application development model, let's review why everybody is so excited about using the Internet infrastructure for application deployment. The most obvious reason the Internet is so interesting is because it gives users remote access to information. More information is available than will ever fit on a client machine. The question then becomes, which model best enables on-demand, source-independent information browsing?

Figure 1 shows the basic client/server model of the Internet. The client provides the presentation context, typically a browser such as Microsoft Internet Explorer or Netscape Navigator that allows remote data to be viewed through the HTML presentation layer. This data represents a slice of the content of the Internet. The network moves the content to the presentation context via HTTP.

URLs further separate the location of content from the presentation context, allowing a browser to access multiple servers and their associated data. Actual access to the content is deferred until the user wants to see it. This deferral mechanism places minimal demands on the network and avoids the transfer of unnecessary data to the client machine. This approach facilitates the exposure of a maximum amount of remote resources with the minimum use of network and client-side resources (see Figure 2).

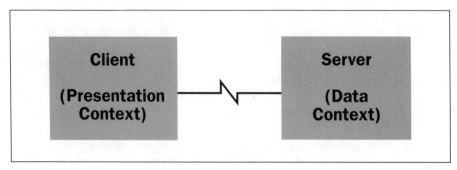

Figure 1: *Client/Server Model.*

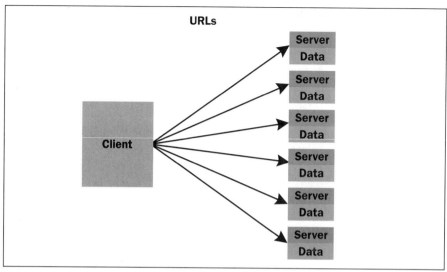

Figure 2: *Remote Data.*

Remote data isn't the only reason why the Internet is interesting—users also want to access logic and services not on their local machines. URLs are as useful as locators for remote logic and services as they are for remote data. It's the combination of data and logic that forms the new content for the Internet. As illustrated in Figure 3, the structure is the same.

The new content for the Internet is objects—specifically, C++ classes that exist on the server. These are the regular kinds of C++ classes you create, edit, compile, and debug with the Visual C++ development environment. Although the current approach to Internet deployment is typically procedural, where the data operates separately from the logic, it can be enhanced with the object-based model you're used to.

ActiveX and Java give application deployment more flexibility. The client becomes a mechanism for accessing remote objects on remote servers (see Figure 4). The server contains data and logical content in program structures such as C++ classes.

How can remote objects best be exposed to the client user over the network infrastructure? The Internet's greatest potential is realized when logic and services, together with content, are presented to multiple users in a context of transparent, real-time collaboration (see Figure 5). Collaboration in a network environment means that two or more users can communicate with one another by viewing or interacting with common data and services. The sessionless nature of the Internet lets multiple clients access an object's state concurrently.

Collaboration on the Internet removes the user's dependency on the location of information and services by allowing many users to interact with information freed from the constraints of monolithic applications. But collaboration in an Internet environment is a particularly difficult task.

The Application Building Litmus Test

So you're convinced that you want to take advantage of the Internet for deploying applications. How can you be sure that the tools you select or the methods you employ for building and publishing your applications are going to yield the best results? Let's develop a litmus test to ensure that the solution you choose will meet your objectives. When building applications for the Internet, ask yourself the following questions: What architectural features mesh most logically with the structure of the Internet? What are the requirements for a development framework to create Internet object-based applications using Visual C++? Why didn't I become an accountant? How can I best use an Internet client/server architecture with the Visual C++ development environment I already use? What is a good Internet application development solution, not just for the Internet of today but into the future?

Let's take a brief look at some of the features you need to get your C++ objects to the Web.

Just Enough Java

An important part of the litmus test is the application-deployment mechanism. Applications should be able to run without needing client software or plug-ins to be installed prior to connection. This dynamic deployment mech-

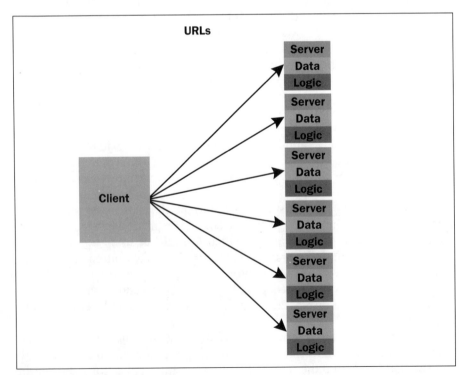

Figure 3: *Remote Data and Logic.*

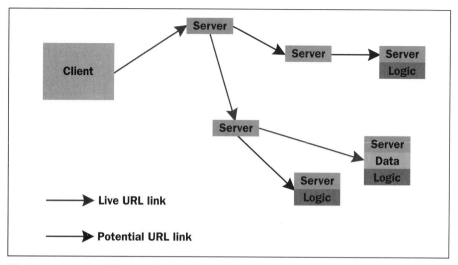

Figure 4: *Remote Object Deployment.*

anism enables all or part of the application to be downloaded to the client machine and run locally, allowing the application to benefit from local machine services such as the display, input devices, and local interactive controls in the user interface. Application performance and interactivity are made possible because code is downloaded and run on the local machine.

What parts of the application really need to be downloaded and run? Certainly not the application logic. Application logic interacts with data not on the client machine (for example, corporate databases, data repositories, and shared information services). In addition, the application logic I'm talking about consists of C++ objects running on the server.

The part of the application that gets downloaded and run on the client machine is the presentation layer. But how do you get the presentation onto the client machine? This presentation layer includes the GUI elements along with just enough application logic to convert user interface events into object state changes. These state changes, and only these state changes, are what your client will send across the Internet to the server.

One way to do this is by using what I call "Just Enough Java." This use of Java is simply pragmatic. Besides providing a dynamic download of the presentation layer, Java offers platform independence, effectively making your Visual C++ applications cross-platform. In addition, as a client-side solution, Java takes advantage of its virtual-machine security model.

Thinner is Better

Thinner is better. No, this isn't an infomercial for the Thighmaster. When it comes to Internet clients, thin is definitely in. The interesting thing about the Internet is that most of the data and logic that users want to access is not on their machines. What do you send down to the client machine to successfully access and deploy an application? Here, less is more. Why? Let's review the fat client problem.

Practically all of the work done with Java to date uses a fat client model. That is, the application logic, not just the presentation layer, is downloaded to the client machine for execution. Why is this a bad approach? First of all, by downloading the application logic to the client, the logic is displaced from the content the user is trying to access. This violates the basic object-oriented model of data/logic encapsulation. The application has to be split, code has to be sent down to the client, and a network protocol has to be created and maintained by the developer. The whole process involves creating a distributed application, greatly increasing the complexity of writing an application simply to move it to the Internet.

Another problem with fat clients is the burden that the application places on the client. If too much of the processing burden takes place on the client machine or device, fewer types of client applications and platforms will be able to access and run that application. This will become a problem when Internet appliances become popular. Cramming a large application into a narrow-bandwidth pipe and into a limited-performance client device inhibits your ability to move your application to the net. The fat client approach is not appropriate when you cannot rely on the power or capability of the client. So,

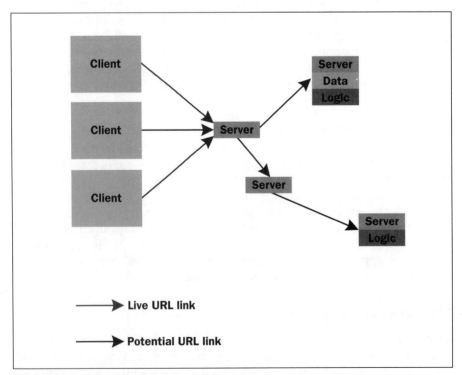

Figure 5: *Real-time Multiple User Collaboration.*

if you've got visions of being able to access your Visual C++ application on a Sega Genesis machine, a cellular phone, or a PDA device, remember: the thinner the client, the fewer restrictions on deploying your application.

Fat clients also suffer because of the bandwidth limitations of the Internet. Since the application logic is on the client in a fat client approach, large amounts of data must be moved to the client machine before the application is able to process it for the user. This movement of data puts an unnecessary bandwidth burden on the network connection. This is problematic because the Internet is largely a low-bandwidth, high-latency environment not conducive to large amounts of network traffic.

Finally, the fat client inhibits collaboration. It becomes a burden to replicate a common state across multiple machines when the application object state is controlled in a distributed fashion. In other words, if the client contains logic that changes a shared object's state, that state must somehow be updated on other clients currently looking at or interacting with that object. This becomes a tremendous burden on the developer. The problem can be remedied somewhat through an RPC or object proxy solution, where multiple clients are accessing centralized data at the server. But client synchronization and data access control are typically left to the developer, since RPC-like mechanisms don't deal with the replication issues associated with collaborative applications.

RPC approaches also include the burden of deciding where to split the application between the client and the server. The developer must write a distributed application where some of the code is Java, JavaScript, or VBScript and the rest is a server object written in C++. Doesn't sound like a very scalable development solution, does it? Besides having to decide which parts of the application are where, the developer has to make coding decisions about what data is changed, whether it is shared or not, and so on. Some technologies attempt to abstract the distributed nature of the application, often requiring the use of a proprietary language, generally resulting in a loss of control over performance issues.

When it comes to deploying applications with the Internet architecture, thinner is better because it allows you to distribute the presentation, not the application. Rapid application access is possible since you do not have to download the entire application. A minimal burden is placed on client resources (or smaller dependency on hardware configuration), and development complexity is reduced because you don't have to write a distributed application. So the litmus test includes a check for thin client Internet application deployment.

Transparent Collaborative Support

Another issue for the litmus test is in the area of collaboration. Collaboration should be a central theme when you talk about the Internet. A Web development effort should not be considered without taking into account how multiple simultaneous users will access that application. Any environment or frame-work should be able to abstract or automate collaborative capability at some level.

I believe that there are two ways in which collaboration can be made possi-ble with minimal developer involvement. The first would be through a code-less presentation model. By codeless I mean that the presentation layer of an application would contain as little application logic as possible (or none) that directly manipulates shared object states. What this means is that object state manipulation code shouldn't be downloaded to the client machine. In an ideal codeless presentation model, the presentation logic executed on the client machine deals only with user interaction (GUI events), transforming those events into data state change commands. Client data state changes should then be packaged and sent to the server to update its objects' states and, in turn, update any other interested clients currently looking at the state of those server objects. The logic that operates on the shared data would be an encap-sulated C++ object running on the server machine. The presentation layer would represent a remote client to that object's services. The central shared object would be accessed by multiple simultaneous clients.

Another collaboration technique allows many clients to have simultaneous dynamic access to a running application. An application framework with such a runtime binding capability could allow clients to attach or detach a particu-lar application during program execution. Since application logic is just another kind of content that can be encountered on the Internet, the same should be the case for applications as well. Runtime binding on an application would allow a client to access an application object's state without involving the shared object directly. By dynamically allowing access to the C++ object, the details for client attachment to that object wouldn't have to be handled by the implementor of the class. This general lack of direct developer involve-ment in the control of collaboration access would greatly simplify the process of writing a multiuser-access Internet app.

State Change-based Client/Server Connection

Available bandwidth has always been a limiting factor for effective deployment of applications over the network, so the litmus test should include an exami-nation of the bandwidth impact.

Where do you divide an application to ensure that the minimum amount of presentation logic is sent to the client and that the application runs opti-mally over the net? The division shouldn't take place at the event level, since many more events occur on the client than are necessary to maintain an appli-cation object's state. Passing events from one side to the other causes the application to create many data round trips before users see the results of their interaction on the screen.

For example, many events happen with a scroll bar interactor, but the important piece of information is the thumb position produced through user interaction. If the scroll bar controls the value of a numeric data member of a C++ object, then only the final scroll bar thumb position value needs to be sent across the network to update the server-side object. This transfer of state information is the minimum information exchange necessary to maintain synchronized application state over a network. To minimize state-transfer bandwidth, you need to send only that part of an application object's semantic state that is currently relevant to the presentation. A core question of GUI research over the last decade has been how best to implement the state transfer.

A model is needed that utilizes the state-based nature intrinsic to object-oriented development. Such a model is essential for optimal communication between the server application and the many clients that can simultaneously access that application. Ideally, the implementation of C++ objects need not be involved directly with this state-change notification scheme. Object state management would then remain external to the application object in the same way a client would access the services of an object without the object being concerned with the details of how it is being used. This approach is appealing because it is not cluttered with unnecessary dependencies such as how the object is used, deployed, accessed, and so on.

Thin Client Three-tier Architecture

The litmus test just created effectively defines a new application architecture for the Internet. This model, which I call the thin client three-tier architecture, can be differentiated from the traditional three-tier client/server approach in two ways. First of all, in the thin client model, all the application-specific logic is running on the server. The logic could be distributed on the server side over many machines, but the approach is inherently server-side. Secondly, in the thin client model, only state changes are exchanged between the client and the server. In the traditional three-tier model the communication between the client and the server is based on remote procedure calls (RPCs). Implementing an application with RPCs requires application-specific logic on the client. Application partitioning is typically left to the developer. The problem with the traditional three-tier architecture with respect to the Internet is that it exhibits many fat client characteristics. It is important to note that a thin client approach allows objects to be accessed by multiple clients simultaneously and in real time.

Traditional client/server approaches, allowing only a single client to access a server process, were OK for the single-user desktop application, but inadequate and too inflexible given the multiclient access capabilities of the Web. Traditionally, multiuser access to data was limited to the multiuser capabilities of the database engine. The thin client approach enables multiuser control of data and services of application objects. The traditional client/server approach controls data and services at the level of the database engine where the context of the data with respect to its associated logic is limited or nonexistent.

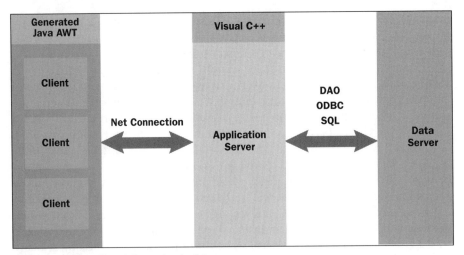

Figure 6: *Thin Client Three-tier Architecture.*

Let's take a look at the implementation of the thin client three-tier architecture. Client, server, and database pieces can be interchangeable. The Java AWT toolkit provides the API for the user interface of an application. The presentation layer (the thin client) can actually be an applet downloaded from the server and run within an Internet browser. The applet contains user-interface widgets such as scroll bars and buttons and enough embedded network communication machinery to respond to and initiate state changes between the client and the server.

A client-side visual element is associated with a specific server-side object. For example, an AWT edit box on the client can be "connected" to a data member of a C++ object running on the server. When a value is typed into the edit box on the client-side applet, a data state change message is sent to the server. In this example, an edit box is a Java applet with a "network" line connected to a server-side object's data member. Any other clients viewing that data member through their interfaces will also update automatically to reflect the object's new state.

Although the client is small, it is also smart enough to know the kind of C++ objects running on the server to which it is connected. The client sends network messages when the user interacts with the AWT control, and receives state changes initiated by the server (for example, when the application logic changes the data member). The generated presentation layer then becomes a client to the server-side C++ objects. The entire client can be generated so that, by default, the developer isn't required to write any code (see Figure 6).

C++ objects are executed on the server. The client download initiates a connection to server objects through an object framework-based protocol. Clients can attach to an already running C++ application on the server or start a unique C++ process upon client-applet startup. Any database accessible through C++ can be accessed by the objects in the server-side application.

Metadata

Having defined the requirements of Internet applications and the architecture necessary to implement them, let me highlight the specific characteristics of a Visual C++ development framework that would enable the creation, deployment, and maintenance of such applications. The framework includes the following capabilities and features: meta data, state change notification, callbacks, runtime binding, cycle reduction, synchronization, and model-view separation. Now, let's take a closer look at each of these components.

Metadata is a format for describing the structure of application objects. In the world of C++, meta data would include information about a class structure, for example, the name of a class, its functions and fields, their types, and so on. The Internet's protocol for discovering the structure of content on the server is HTML. The HTML format couples content and meta data for remote information access. HTTP makes requests on parts of the server content by performing a GET command. The argument of the GET command (the path to the HTML file of interest) is really information about the data the user is trying to access—the meta data. Ideally, application objects are viewed and manipulated over the Internet by accessing them through what I like to call a meta interface.

An effective framework for accessing C++ objects over the Web should be inherently self-describing. In other words, clients are able to access objects' services and structures to attach to these objects. A protocol similar to HTTP incorporated into the framework would enable applet clients to perform application-level GET commands for accessing server-side C++ objects. This same protocol would also support server-side pushes that move C++ object state changes to the client when the object state changed. Meta information is the glue that enables remote presentation to attach to C++ objects on the server.

State Change Notification

While meta information provides remote access, a physical network connection must exist to communicate state changes between the client and the server. State change notification capability must be supported at the framework level. A framework that requires the developer to explicitly deal with data change notification messages adds too much complexity to the application code and places too many dependencies on the details of remote presentation access into the application logic, making application objects inherently non-reusable.

Callbacks

Callbacks are functions called when data changes. C++ provides hooks for allowing functions to be called when data changes in a way that is transparent to the implementor of a class. Suppose the following class represents a way to store and manipulate an *x, y* position:

```
class Point {
public:
 Point(int x, int y) : xPos(x), yPos(y) { }
 void offset(int x, int y) { xPos += x; yPos += y; }
 void setXPos(int x) { xPos = x; }
 void setYPos(int y) { yPos = y; }
 int getXPos() { return xPos; }
 int getYPos() { return yPos; }

private:
 int xPos;
 int yPos;
};
```

The xPos and yPos data members represent the actual information of the
Point class. These data members can have "guarded" or write barrier access
(an Eiffel language term) or they can be "computed fields" (as in Smalltalk).
Each of these implementations fires a callback when data changes. Another
technique, C++ operator overloading, allows code to be executed whenever an
explicit assignment to the data member is performed.

Let's first introduce a new class and then modify the Point class shown
above to include write barrier capability. The following IntData class represents a partial encapsulation of the int type:

```
class IntData {
public:
 Int(int d) { data = d; }
 int operator () { return data; }
 operator = (IntData &d) {}
 operator = (int d) { }

 addCallback(void f(int));
 removeCallback(void f(int));
protected:
 dataChanged()
private:
 int data;
};
```

Now, let's modify the Point class to have callback-enabled data members:

```
class Point {
public:
 Point(int x, int y) : xPos(x), yPos(y) { }
 void offset(int x, int y) { xPos += x; yPos += y; }
 void setXPos(int x) { xPos = x; }
 void setYPos(int y) { yPos = y; }
 int getXPos() { return xPos; }
 int getYPos() { return yPos; }

private:
 IntData xPos;   // CHANGED
 IntData yPos;   // CHANGED
};
```

Notice that the only code in the class that needed to change (as indicated with comments) is the declaration representation of the Point data members, using IntData as the type. Using this mechanism, when a Point object's state changes, clients external to the class can be notified. You'll see a little later that client access to data members can be reasonably restricted to a limited set of clients, for example, clients that visually represent the object remotely. Not just anyone can access the internal state of an object.

This capability allows callbacks to be associated with the state of objects. For brevity, many of the details of encapsulated access have been left out. This method can be applied to C++ object pointers, arrays, reference-counted objects, and so on. This approach to data change notification contributes to a dramatic reduction in the complexity associated with connecting a remote thin client user interface to the object itself. Data members, then, use a "plug and socket" access approach that allows the representation of the object to be external to the implementation of the class.

Runtime Binding

Data change notification is not quite enough. Suppose that clients want to modify the object during program execution without generating code. Code generation complicates the task of attaching multiple heterogeneous clients to server objects. For maximum flexibility in attaching collaborative clients to an object over the Web, a runtime binding mechanism can be added to C++ object access. C++ runtime binding doesn't degrade the general performance of the running object itself. Remember the advantages of having metadata information available to describe the structure of classes? Well, it can also help automate the runtime binding of compiled C++ classes. The metadata of each class that is to be accessible over the Internet can be used to generate a C

```
class Color {
public:
 Color(int r, int g, int b) : red(r), green(g), blue(b) {}
 int getRed() { return red; }
 int getGreen() { return green; }
 int getBlue() { return blue; }
 void setRed(int r) { red = r; }
 void setGreen(int g) { green = g; }
 void setBlue(int b) { blue = b; }

private:
 // "callback enabled" data members
 IntData red;
 IntData green;
 IntData blue;
};
```

Figure 7: *Using Metadata with Runtime Binding.*

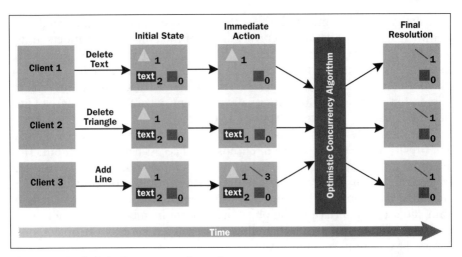

Figure 8: *Optimistic Concurrency Control.*

structure that enables lookup and access to data members of an object by name (for flexibility) and by index (for speed). Of course, the name can be resolved to an offset index at runtime as an optimization.

In Figure 7 the class represents color, which contains red, green, and blue components. Runtime binding access on member functions is also possible, which can further separate the client presentation from the structure of the object. The runtime binding approach allows you to preserve the performance capability of the C++ object itself while allowing remote dynamic access to the object. All this is possible without introducing appreciable complexity for the class implementor (since the runtime binding structure can be automatically generated using the metadata of the class). This lets you focus on the business logic without concern for the details of making the object's state externally viewable.

Cycle Reduction

When monitoring data changes on objects, cycles can occur that would cause infinite callback conditions. For example, the following doTransaction function gets called:

```
void doTransaction()
{
    A = 10;
}
```

A callback function, AChanged(int a), was added to the callback list on the A member so that, when A is assigned to 10, the AChanged function is called:

```
void AChanged(int a)
{
    B = 20;
}
```

A callback function, BChanged, was in turn added to the B data member, and so it is called as well.

```
void BChanged(int b)
{
    doTransaction();
}
```

Notice that the BChanged function calls the same function that started the chain of functions to be called in the first place. This creates an infinite cycle. Unless reduced, this sequence of changes and notifications will happen at a furious pace so long as the system stack will permit. The solution is to set a flag so that if the data change callback notification happens while that same data is being changed, the callback function isn't called again.

Synchronization

Concurrency control always becomes an issue when dealing with multiple threads of execution. In the thin client three-tier model, multiple clients can update the state of shared objects on the server at the same time. How do you resolve synchronization problems as they occur without coding the concurrency control into the objects themselves? Keep in mind that simple proxy methodologies or RPC mechanisms don't handle concurrency issues automatically. A remote function call that changes an object's state can corrupt or break other clients making similar requests on the same object at the same time.

Let's look at a fairly simple example. Suppose a virtual whiteboard object is running on the server. It contains a list of shapes that have been drawn on the whiteboard by several remote thin clients. The current state of the whiteboard includes a square (item 0), triangle (item 1), and a line of text (item 2). Three clients are currently viewing the whiteboard. Client 1 invokes a command to

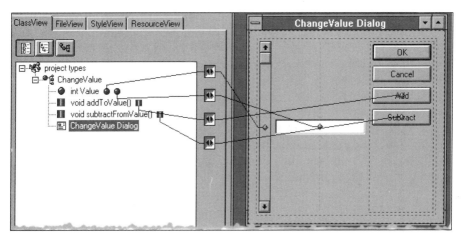

Figure 9: *Presentation Decoupling.*

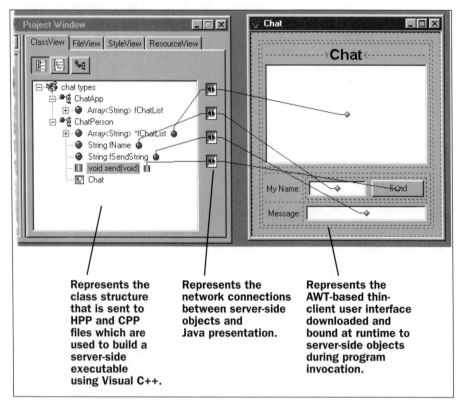

Figure 10: *Chat Applet in Development.*

delete the text (item 2). At the same time client 2 invokes a command to delete the triangle shape (item 1). Also at the same time, client 3 sends a command to add a line. Without concurrency control, the object state will depend on the order in which the commands are handled by the server object.

Here's an example of how optimistic concurrency control resolves this problem (see Figure 8). Let's say the server handles or sees the "delete the triangle" (item 1) first. The delete command is performed successfully. Next, the server processes the command to delete the text (item 2). Of course, by now the previous delete of the 0th item could corrupt the intent of deleting item 2. The second delete command needs its index to be decreased by one to index 1 (a transformation) to preserve the intent of the command (deleting the text item). Finally, the third command to add a line at the end of the shape list needs no modification since the index of the line item depends on what is currently the last item index. The key to making this scenario work correctly is to use an optimistic algorithm that preserves object states. It is an optimistic approach because no client-to-server negotiation takes place to resolve state change commands. The algorithm assumes that commands can be transformed as they are encountered to preserve the object's integrity. In Figure 8, the immediate action on the whiteboard is translated into the final resolution by the optimistic algorithm.

The concurrency control example given above is specific to array or list-based data structures. Each data type requires a unique set of rules appropriate to it. Typically, a temporal list is maintained to monitor and adjust operations on data structures based on the data type's rules. Commands from the clients can be transformed to preserve the integrity of the transaction. Again, this synchronization capability can exist outside of the regular implementation of application-specific C++ classes if runtime binding and data change callbacks are integral to the object structure or framework.

Complete Presentation Decoupling

In the thin client architecture, user interfaces visually represent objects running on the server. In an ideal environment, the presentation is separated from the objects themselves. Figure 9 illustrates the point.

In Figure 9, a class (ChangeValue) contains a single data member (value) and two functions (addToValue and subtractFromValue). This ClassView tool is part of the framework package available electronically. The ChangeValue class, when instantiated at runtime, will execute on the server. A dialog can be created that visually represents the entire class. The scroll bar and the edit box are both client controls attached to the class member int value. The buttons control the direct invocation of the member functions of the class. The lines shown between the client presentation and the server C++ object represent the state change management relationship that exists between the thin client and the server-based application object.

```
// chatApp.h
class ChatApp: public EosFramework
{
public:
ChatApp();
ChatApp(const ChatApp& src);
virtual ~ChatApp();
ChatApp& operator =(const ChatApp& src);

    // overriden functions from the base application framework class
    virtual EosObject  *getFirstObject();
    virtual EosAtom  getClientViewName(EosClient *client);

private:
// storage for the chat strings based on messages created by remote clients
    EosPrimitiveArray<EosString> fChatList;
};
```

Figure 11: chatApp.h

```
// chatApp.cpp
#include "stdeos.hpp"
#include <chatApp.h>
#include <chatperson.h>

// retrieves a chat person object for each client that attaches to the
            server .exe
EosObject *ChatApp::getFirstObject()
{
  return (EosObject *)new ChatPerson(&fChatList);
}
// allows the server app to control the object and dialog name that is to
            be used at the applet level
// of the remote presentation
EosAtom ChatApp::getClientViewName(EosClient *client)
{
  return EosAtom("ChatPerson.Chat");
}

// misc. member functions
ChatApp::ChatApp() : EosFramework(),
    fChatList()
{
}
ChatApp::ChatApp(const ChatApp& src) : EosFramework(src),
    fChatList(src.fChatList)
{
}
ChatApp::~ChatApp()
{
}
ChatApp& ChatApp::operator =(const ChatApp& src)
{
    if (this != &src)
    {
        EosFramework::operator=(src);
        fChatList = src.fChatList;
    }
    return *this;
}
```

Figure 12: chatApp.cpp

In this example, the user would look at the presentation embedded in the HTML page as a Java applet. The object (the effective content for the client presentation) is manipulated as the user interacts with the thin client interface. For example, suppose the user presses the Add button. This causes the

```
// chatperson.hpp
class ChatPerson: public EosObject
{
public:
ChatPerson();
ChatPerson(const ChatPerson& src);
virtual ~ChatPerson();
ChatPerson& operator =(const ChatPerson& src);

    // constructor which initializes the shared chat list
  ChatPerson(EosPrimitiveArray<EosString> *chatList);

// adds the user message to the chat list
  void send(void);

protected:
    // client message string for adding to the chat list
    EosString fSendString;
    // the client user name to be presented with the client's message
          in the chat list
  EosString fName;
    // a "reference" to the shared chat list initialized within the
          ChatPerson constructor
  EosPrimitiveArrayRef<EosString> fChatList;
};
```

Figure 13: chatperson.hpp

client to initiate a command to call the member function addToValue on the
ChangeValue class. The following code is written for the addToValue function:

```
void ChangeValue::addToValue()
{
 // change the value, this may create callbacks to occurs depending
 // on the number of clients currently interested in this value
 value += 10;
}
```

The value change will produce a set of callbacks to be invoked, which will subsequently update any thin clients currently attached to the ChangeValue
object, including the scroll bar and edit box shown on the page where the user
pressed the button.

Sample Application

My thin client Internet sample application uses C++ code on the server and a
Java applet running in Internet Explorer on the client. This basic chat program comprises only a few pages of code but manages to show the collabora-

tion capability inherent in server-centric architectures. The program allows users to add messages to a chat listing that all attached clients can see in real time. Clients add to the common list by typing in the message and invoking a send command. Users can identify themselves via an edit string. Clients are dynamically attached to and detached from a running server-based chat

```cpp
// chatperson.cpp
#include "stdeos.hpp"
#include <chatperson.hpp>

// performs the send which adds the client string to the chat list
void ChatPerson::send()
{
  // prepare the client string and add it to the chat list
  EosString theString("(" + fName + ") " + fSendString);
  fChatList->add(theString);

  // now clear the send string field on the client
  fSendString = "";
}

// the constructor that takes a reference to the global chat list
ChatPerson::ChatPerson(EosPrimitiveArray<EosString> *chatList) :
            EosObject(),
    fSendString(),
    fName(),
      // assign the shared chat list object with this client
      fChatList(chatList) {}

ChatPerson::ChatPerson() : EosObject(),
    fSendString(),
    fName(),
    fChatList() {}
ChatPerson::ChatPerson(const ChatPerson& src) : EosObject(src),
    fSendString(src.fSendString),
    fName(src.fName),
    fChatList(src.fChatList) {}
ChatPerson::~ChatPerson() {}
ChatPerson& ChatPerson::operator =(const ChatPerson& src)
{
    if (this != &src)
    {
        EosObject::operator=(src);
        fSendString = src.fSendString;
        fName = src.fName;
        fChatList = src.fChatList;
    }
    return *this;
}
```

Figure 14: cchatperson.cpp

application. While all clients share the common chat list, other information is client-specific and is invisible to other users. The application structure along with the Java client presentation is first defined in the Internet-enabled app builder, part of my framework (see Figure 10).

The C++ class definitions are defined in the builder, which uses class schema information to build connections to the Java-based dialogs. As the class structure and the Java client dialogs are designed, the application developer invokes the commands to generate the basic pieces for deploying an Internet application. On the server side, basic C++ skeleton code is created by the builder (the .h and .cpp files for the classes defined in the builder). On the client side, a Java applet is generated and automatically compiled by the builder prior to deployment to the client in the context of an HTML page. As a convenience, a Visual C++ .mak file is generated so that the server side application compiles to an .exe. The application developer then implements the app-specific logic in the member functions of the classes and compiles the app directly. Code editing, debugging, and general development all take place in the familiar Visual C++ environment. On the client side, there is no more code to write. By default, an HTML file is generated for each project created in the application builder environment. The Java applet is simply referenced in an HTML file and automatically runs when the user double-clicks on the reference. Let's first look at the C++ code you would write.

Server Side C++ Code

Two classes are defined in the builder: ChatApp and ChatPerson. ChatApp is derived from my EosFramework, which provides basic application-level procedures. You can think of the EosFramework class as the main() of the server side application. It has functions that control various program aspects: collaboration control, application startup and shutdown, and so on. An array of strings is defined in the ChatApp class that represents all the messages sent by the various clients since the application started (see ChatApp::fChatList in Figure 11). The EosPrimitiveArray class is templated for string types and uses the MFC CArray class for its storage and basic functionality. The fChatList data member of ChatApp defines the data that is to be shared among all attached clients. Two other functions, getFirstObject and getClientViewName, are used for controlling multiple collaborative clients (see Figure 11).

The chat application is launched for the first time when a Java thin client applet requests access to the server-based application. Since this application is designed to be collaborative, each new client attaches to the same chat application process running on the server. The rules regarding client to server connections can be defined by the developer, including attaching a single server process to multiple clients or attaching only one client to a server process. In the application example, I want each client that attaches to the chat process to receive its own private object. This object, ChatPerson, allows the user to view common data (the chat list) as well as its own uniquely viewed information. The function ChatApp::getFirstObject is called at runtime whenever a new

```
// Java File Generated By ViewSoft's Builder
// Portions Copyright (c) 1996 MSJ
package chat;
import java.applet.*;
import java.awt.*;
import java.util.*;
import viewsoft.*;
public class ChatPerson extends EosEmbeddedView
{
  // this section of the generated code is used for client/server
            communication
  // and basic object to dialog connections...
  // socket port used for remote server side communication private
            EosPort fPort;
  // information used to connect view to C++ object on the server
  private EosMapperTable fIdTable;
  public ChatPerson() { super(); init(); }

  // data state change management hooks
  public EosMapperTableEntry getProbe(int id)
  { return (EosMapperTableEntry) fIdTable.elementAt(id); }
  public void removeProbe(int id) { fIdTable.removeProbe(id); }
  public void setMapperTable(EosMapperTable table) { fIdTable = table; }

  // port assignment
  public void setPort(EosPort port) { fPort = port; }

  // "resource" generation for the ChatPerson object dialogs designed in
            the
  // builder... responds to applet request to create an instance of a
  // ChatPerson dialog
  public void createView(String viewName, Container shell)
  {
    // since an object can have multiple views a comparison is made when
            the
    // create view function is called
    if (viewName.equals("Chat"))
    {
      int id;

      // create a geometry layout manager
      EosBoxContainer eosC1 = new EosBoxContainer();
      this.add(eosC1);

      // propagate communication variables
      eosC1.setPort(fPort);
      eosC1.setMapperTable(fIdTable);
      EosBoxContainer eosC2 = new EosBoxContainer();
      eosC1.add(eosC2);
      eosC2.setPort(fPort);
```

Figure 15: *Java Thin Client Chat Applet.*

Figure 15: *Java Thin Client Chat Applet, continued.*

```
        eosC2.setMapperTable(fIdTable);

        // add the "Chat" label
        EosLabel eosC3 = new EosLabel();
        eosC2.add(eosC3);
        eosC3.setProperty("Caption", new EosString("Chat"));

        // add the list box for the chat list
        EosListBox eosC4 = new EosListBox();
        eosC2.add(eosC4);

        // probe ids...used to connect dialog elements to the object
                running on
        // the server
        id = fIdTable.attachProbe(eosC4, "fInvalidate");
        eosC4.setUp(fPort, "fInvalidate", id);
        id = fIdTable.attachProbe(eosC4, "select");
        eosC4.setUp(fPort, "select", id);
        id = fIdTable.attachProbe(eosC4, "insert");
        eosC4.setUp(fPort, "insert", id);
        id = fIdTable.attachProbe(eosC4, "fRemove");
        eosC4.setUp(fPort, "fRemove", id);
        id = fIdTable.attachProbe(eosC4, "fRemoveAll");
        eosC4.setUp(fPort, "fRemoveAll", id);
        id = fIdTable.attachProbe(eosC4, "set");
        eosC4.setUp(fPort, "set", id);

        // create a row/column layout manager
        EosGridContainer eosC5 = new EosGridContainer();
        eosC1.add(eosC5);

        // propagate communication variables
        eosC5.setPort(fPort);
        eosC5.setMapperTable(fIdTable);

        // "My Name" label
        EosLabel eosC6 = new EosLabel();
        eosC5.add(eosC6);
        eosC6.setProperty("Caption", new EosString("My Name:"));

        // horizontal layout manager
        EosBoxContainer eosC7 = new EosBoxContainer();
        eosC5.add(eosC7);
        eosC7.setPort(fPort);
        eosC7.setMapperTable(fIdTable);

        // user name edit box
        EosTextField eosC8 = new EosTextField();
        eosC7.add(eosC8);
        // probe ids
```

Figure 15: *Java Thin Client Chat Applet, continued.*

```
        id = fIdTable.attachProbe(eosC8, "fText");
        eosC8.setUp(fPort, "fText", id);

        // send button
        EosButton eosC9 = new EosButton();
        eosC7.add(eosC9);
        // probe ids
        id = fIdTable.attachProbe(eosC9, "fPressed");
        eosC9.setUp(fPort, "fPressed", id);
        eosC9.setProperty("Caption", new EosString("Send"));

        // "Message" label
        EosLabel eosC10 = new EosLabel();
        eosC5.add(eosC10);
        eosC10.setProperty("Caption", new EosString("Message:"));

        // edit box for the client message
        EosTextField eosC11 = new EosTextField();
        eosC5.add(eosC11);
        // probe ids
        id = fIdTable.attachProbe(eosC11, "fText");
        eosC11.setUp(fPort, "fText", id);
    }
  }
 }
```

client attaches to the server's running process. It returns the first object that will be presented to the user as a Java applet. The state of the data associated with the ChatPerson instance will be automatically reflected in the Java applet user interface based on the dialog that was designed for that object in the application builder. The function ChatApp::getClientViewName (see Figure 12) allows the developer to control exactly which dialog designed in the builder will be initially presented to the user on the client.

The ChatPerson object will actually be presented to the client remotely in the Java applet. One instance of ChatPerson is created for each client that attaches to the chat application. When the client detaches from the server side application, its ChatPerson instance will be deleted as well.

The basic framework defined here allows the developer to define C++ object pointer members with a reference-counted template wrapper class. This class is useful for determining when an object is no longer interesting to other parties. This is especially useful in the case when clients attach and detach at runtime. When a client detaches from the server process, and if that client held the only reference to the object, it will automatically go out of scope. This greatly reduces object pointer management often associated with C++ based applications. The ChatPerson member fChatList is another example of automatic reference counting. A reference to the global chat list is assigned to the client in order for the ChatPerson object to attach client-specific messages. Only when the actual application terminates does the global chat list go out of scope, since its count is the number of active clients (ChatPerson instances) plus the ChatApp ownership of the array.

Additional members of ChatPerson include a string for creating the message to send (fSendString), the name of the client sending the message (fName), and a send function that prepares the string and adds it to the global chat list (see Figures 13 and 14).

Just a few lines of code are required to perform the basic chat application functionality. Notice that in this object connection-based approach the code that deals with application-specific logic (that of manipulating class members, and so on) doesn't have to concern itself with network connections, sockets or RPC-based code, Java AWT client control settings, or communication. Those pieces are decoupled from the class structure itself and are automatically resolved by the connection technology enabled by the builder.

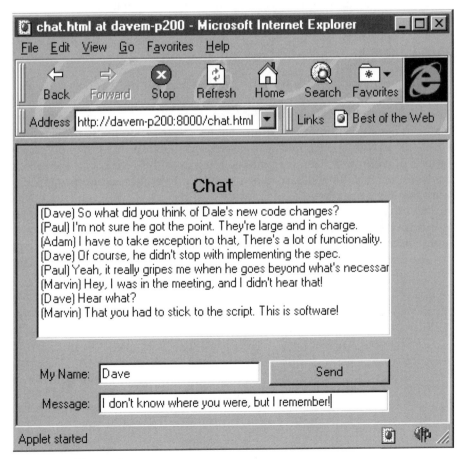

Figure 16: *Chat applet.*

The Java Generated Client

Although by default the details of the Java client applet (see Figure 15) are hidden by the builder's code generation, it is useful to look at the client code to see better what is happening there. Comments added to the generated code indicate the various pieces incorporated on the client in order to present and access remote C++ objects running on the server. It should be noted that some generated code has been omitted for brevity. A full example of the application can be inspected at http://www.viewsoft.com/examples or on the CD-ROM.

There are three main pieces to the Java applet that are generated to successfully deploy Internet thin-clients attached to C++ server executables. These are: socket communication, dialog resource description and creation, and remote C++ member attachment and connection protocols. These three components work in concert to create a Java applet that has minimal client-side resource requirements while still providing optimal communication performance over various Internet access speeds.

Figure 16 demonstrates the client view of the chat application running in Internet Explorer.

Summary

To summarize, the thin client three-tier model builds on your expertise as a Visual C++ developer for creating powerful applications for the Internet. The model lets you effectively use Java, giving your applications the dynamic cross-platform deployment mechanism needed for the Internet. It also provides the client side of your applications with just enough application logic to optimally process and communicate user interaction across the Internet to the server. And, best of all, you don't have to be a Java guru to build real Internet applications that solve real problems with Java.

The excitement surrounding the Internet is here to stay. The challenge to you is to apply the litmus test as you evaluate the profusion of frameworks and tools available in the months ahead. Then, while everyone else is trying to figure out which way they're going, you can get some real work done.

Developing JDBC Applications

Andrew Wilson

The JDBC allows Java developers to create applications that can attach and interact with a variety of databases. On PCs, a JDBC application must load a "bridge" that communicates between the JDBC code and an ODBC driver. This bridge is a DLL and is the key to making any PC-based JDBC applet work.

The JDBC applet has a few lines of code that load the driver and cast the resulting class to the JDBC's driver class. The driver is then used to establish connections to various databases, send SQL statements, and gather results. The JDBC provides the same level of database functionality you would expect from tools such as Borland's Delphi and Microsoft's Visual Basic.

There are a few significant advantages that applets have over applications. One is that applets can be executed by browsing a web page; thus, you can make modifications without having the user reinstall. In fact, users need never install anything beyond their browser software. This gives you the ability to make code changes without having to redistribute the application or reinstall.

However, many JDBC developers have run into a strange problem. JDBC applets cannot be loaded from browsers like Netscape's Navigator or Microsoft's Internet Explorer because they cannot load the driver—the method for invoking the DLL is simply incompatible.

Andrew is an engineer for NuMega Technologies in Nashua, NH. Reprinted courtesy of Dr. Dobb's Sourcebook.

The inability to browse JDBC applets on the PC is a significant roadblock, but there is a way around it. Instead of directly loading an applet that attaches to a database, you can develop two separate applets—a server that establishes the connection to the database, and a client that communicates with the server. This lets you browse the client applet, giving you the same database connectivity without having to install any special drivers on a user's system.

The Model

Both the client and the server use a series of network support classes found in the java.net package. The client will use the *Socket* class to establish a connection on the server (which is listening by way of the *ServerSocket* class). However, the client applet has a significant limitation: It can only communicate with the same system that sent the applet. If the client applet was loaded from server Wombat, the applet can only attach back to Wombat. It may not attach to any other system because of applet-security restrictions. This means that you must run the database server on the same system as the web server.

The database server starts by trying to load the JDBC driver and establish a connection. Once the connection has been made, the server spawns a new thread to listen for incoming client connections. When a client attaches, a new thread, which will interact with the user and act as a session manager, is generated.

To make this work, both the client and the server must be able to speak the same language, so you must produce a new class that organizes the requests of the client into something that can be read by the server. Obviously, the class must also be able to take the server's replies and convert them into something the client can understand.

This adds a convenient layer of abstraction. The client never really knows what is passing the information back to it. The server could be a Java, C/C++, or even a Visual Basic application. The client only knows that it is receiving data in the correct format. The server could communicate with a client written in any language: The only important component is the protocol used to communicate (which you customize to fit your needs).

Once the client has attached and the session manager is active, users can make any query or update. The server simply interprets the incoming packet and generates the correct SQL code on the fly. Once the SQL statement has been executed, the server passes back the resulting data in the correct format by way of the protocol manager.

The Implementation

To illustrate this model, I've written a complete Java database server and client applet. They were coded in Microsoft's Visual J++ and recompiled and tested using Javasoft's JDK. The project is called "Call Tracker." It's a simple tracking system that lets users create, update, and view customer calls to a technical-support group. The complete source code and related files are available on the CD-ROM.

The server is broken down into four classes. The first is CTRCKRSVR, which is extended from the *Applet* class and implements the runable interface. This class generates the user interface and establishes the connection with the database. Once the connection has been established, the server starts an instance of *ServerThread*.

The connection to the database is seen in Listing One. It starts by trying to load the JDBC-ODBC bridge. The *JdbcOdbcDriver* class dynamically loads the JdbcOdbc.dll and creates a new *Driver* instance. Once you have the driver running, you should determine if the driver follows the JDBC specification. You then confirm that it can attach to the database prior to actually attaching. This is done by specifying the ODBC driver's URL, where *m_JDBCUrl* is *"jdbc:odbc:"+m_DBName*. *m_DBName* can be any string that names a system data source. We finally attach to the database via *m_Connection = DriverManager.getConnection (m_JDBCUrl);* which establishes the connection and gives us full access to the database.

The *Connection* class is the framework for the generation of SQL statements and the gathering of results. It specifies how and when data is written to the database. You can use it to find the names of various tables in the database, as well as the state of the database. It finally determines how data is written when the connection is closed. Note that a *Connection* should be closed when it is no longer being used (formally breaking the link to the database).

Listing Two shows the *run* member of the CTRCKRSVR class. It executes the *startServices()* function in Listing One. It also kicks off a new instance of *ServerThread*. It uses three parameters in its constructor. The first is the socket that the server should listen to. The second is an instance of the *Connection* class (initialized in *startServices()*). The third is a list class (*m_Log*) that acts as a list box. The *m_Log* member is used throughout the server to act as a log of activities. Anytime a user attaches or makes a query or an update, it is displayed in that list. Finally, the class updates a label repeatedly to show the time and date.

ServerThread listens for incoming client connections. The class is an extended *Thread* class. Thus, at its creation, it begins executing separately from the main application's thread. Listing Three shows the key members. The *run* member calls *InitServer* to initialize the *ServerSocket* class that listens for a connection. *m_Server.accept()* causes the socket to go into a blocking state until an application tries to connect to the socket. Once a connection occurs, *m_Server.accept()* returns a new *Socket* class that is used as a part of the *Session* class' constructor. Note that you also pass in the log and connection members. Further, the thread literally stops until a connection is made. This construct is fairly important: It makes it possible to have many users attach and interact with the database at the same time.

The *Session* class is responsible for communication between the client and the server, translating the incoming packets (by way of the *TrackerData* class), and acting upon them by executing a query, update, or insert, and then passing the results back to the client. The constructor is responsible for establishing the data-stream classes and starting the execution of the thread; see Listing Four.

Note that you are using a stream-based transport (TCP). There are a number of reasons for using this over datagram (UDP) communication. Streams work in the same way a file stream would operate. You simply read from the stream until you get an EOF or an exception occurs. Stream-based communication is typically used for passing files or large blocks of data. The stream is able to manage splitting data across multiple packets as well as reassembly (this is important, since a name or a problem in our call-tracking system can be any length). You don't need to concern yourself with how the network passes the data. Further, TCP adds several checks that confirm data arrival and check for data corruption.

The *run()* member is really just a *while* loop that constantly calls *manageConnection()*. As is shown in Listing Five, *manageConnection()* does many different things. It starts by getting the current time. When the minute value changes, you send a "heartbeat" packet, testing the socket and confirming that the client is still attached (an exception is thrown if the user dropped the connection, closing the data streams and the socket). *manageConnection()* also terminates the thread. The client doesn't interpret the heartbeat, it just cleans the incoming stream and waits for new data.

You call *m_InStream.available()* to see if there is any data in the incoming data stream that can be read. *m_InStream.readFully(stream)* then reads the contents of the stream into a buffer, which is used to build a *TrackerData* object. *TrackerData* parses the string into the various data types or fields used in the database. Then *TrackerData.getType()* is called to determine the kind of data you received (update, insert, query, and so on).

ID is used to determine if the database function ran correctly. All records in the database are given a unique number. You can use this to determine if the SQL statement was successful. If it is, the record's ID is returned, otherwise you receive a −1. After each transaction, you return the record to the client with the ID.

Now take a look at the code that inserts a new row into the database. Listing Six begins with *addDBItem(TrackerData)*, which first confirms that there were first- and last-name values entered. It then attaches to the database by calling *attachDB()*, which creates a new instance of the JDBC's *Statement* class.

The *Statement* class is used to perform all SQL statement operations (barring prepared statements handled by the *Connection* class). This includes insert, delete, and query operations. Results gathered by queries are returned in the *RecordSet* class.

BuildRecordString() is used to get the new entry's fields. The resulting string is prepended with the SQL statement that performs the insert operation. You then pass the SQL statement into *statement.executeUpdate(SQLStatement)* and close the statement object. Note that *statement.executeUpdate(SQLStatement)* handles both updates and inserts. An exception is thrown if the operation fails, at which point you try to close the SQL statement again to terminate the object correctly.

Queries are not much more difficult. Listing Seven shows *getID()*, which does a query to get the ID of a record that was recently added or updated. This function confirms that the record was actually written and returns its ID. A –1 is returned if the function fails. *getID()* starts by attaching to the database and establishing a statement object. It then executes a SQL statement that returns the affected row. The statement *rs = statement.executeQuery(SQLStatement);* runs the query and returns a *ResultSet* object. You then move to the first row of the result set and display the first field in the record. You do this by calling *rs.getInt(1)*, which will return the integer form of the record's row number. Both the *ResultSet* and *Statement* objects are closed and the ID is returned. If either the query or the *RecordSet* failed, an exception is thrown and an error will be added to the log.

The last part of the server is the *TrackerData* class (Listing Eight). This class is shared by both the server and the client. It is responsible for formatting the various fields into a single string. The class can also take a string and break it down into the fields that make up a record. It includes the type identifier, length of the next data item, and data item itself. Each item is separated by a dash. The length of each data item is critical (since a dash may also be used in the data item).

An incoming string is parsed by creating a new *TrackerData* with that string. You then call *parsePacket()*, which breaks the string down based upon the type field. The individual fields are retrieved by calling the *getXXX()* member, where *XXX* is the field name. This allows the remainder of the applet, be it client or server, to remain unaware of the stream's construction.

Outgoing strings are built in a similar fashion. First, the *TrackerData* object is created. Next, the various fields are populated by calling the *setXXX()*, where *XXX* is the field name. The *buildPacket()* is then called, returning the string that is to be sent to the network. (See Listing Nine.)

The client is little more than a user interface. It is downloaded from the web site and executed through the browser. It attempts to attach to the JDBC server, then passes new records or queries by building the appropriate string through the *TrackerData* class and forwarding it to the server. An incoming string is broken down through the *TrackerData* class and the fields are displayed in the appropriate user-interface object.

Conclusion

The JDBC is fairly easy to work with. However, writing applications where the JDBC can be used effectively is obviously much more complicated. The client/server design allows users to run database applications by simply browsing the applet without having any special drivers that would normally be needed to attach and interact with a database. The key is that the JDBC server can attach to the database, and the client can attach to the server.

You can now produce robust Internet database applications that can offer customers, telecommuters, and employees access to the information they need without having to set up special dial-in accounts or extra leased-line connections. Further, one application can communicate with the server regardless of platform, virtually eliminating the need to write applications for any particular operating system in the database arena.

Listing One

```
Driver  m_JDBCDriver;
String  m_JDBCUrl;
Connection m_Connection;

public boolean StartServices ()
    {
        try
        {
            m_JDBCDriver  =(Driver) Class.forName
              ("jdbc.odbc.JdbcOdbcDriver").newInstance();  // Loads JDBC driver
            if ( !m_JDBCDriver.jdbcCompliant () )
            {
                m_Log.addItem ( "Driver is not JDBC compliant");
                return false;
            }
            if (m_JDBCDriver.acceptsURL ( m_JDBCUrl ) )
                                    // Confirms that we can attach to this URL
            {
                m_Log.addItem ( "Trying to establish a
                                            connection with "+m_JDBCUrl);
                m_Connection = DriverManager.getConnection ( m_JDBCUrl );
                return true;
            }
        } catch (ClassNotFoundException e)
        {
            m_Log.addItem ( "Could not load JDBC-ODBC bridge,
                                            check your path env.");
            m_Log.addItem ( e.getMessage() );
            return false;
        }
        catch (SQLException db)
        {
            m_Log.addItem ( "Connection failed: " +db.getMessage());
        }
        catch (Exception e)
        {
            m_Log.addItem ( "Critical Fault in Starting DB services");
            m_Log.addItem ( e.getMessage() );
        }
        return false;
    }
```

Listing Two

```
List m_Log;
Label m_TimeLabel;
int m_Port;

public void run()
    {
        StartServices();
        m_ServerThread = new ServerThread ( m_Port, m_Connection, m_Log );
        m_Log.addItem ( "Database driver and socket services are up" );
        while (true)
        {
            m_TimeLabel.setText( new Date().toString() );
        }
    }
```

Listing Three

```
protected ServerSocket m_Server = null;
protected Session m_Session = null;

protected void InitServer ()
{
    if (m_Server == null)
    {
        try
        {
            m_Server = new ServerSocket ( m_Port, 6 );
            m_Log.addItem ( "Socket server is up at port: " + m_Port );
            m_Log.makeVisible ( m_Log.countItems ()  - 1);
        } catch ( IOException e)
        {
            m_Log.addItem ( "Could not create socket:" + m_Port );
            m_Log.addItem ( e.getMessage() );
            m_Log.makeVisible ( m_Log.countItems ()  - 1);
            Stop ();
        }
    }
}
public void run ()
{
    InitServer ();
    while (true)
    {
        try
        {
            m_Log.addItem ( "Waiting for Connect" );
            m_Session = new Session (m_Server.accept(), m_Connection, m_Log);
            m_Log.addItem ( "User has attached" );
            m_Log.makeVisible ( m_Log.countItems ()  - 1);
        } catch ( IOException e)
        {
            m_Log.addItem ( "Could not Accept" + m_Port );
```

```
                    m_Log.addItem ( e.getMessage() );
                    m_Log.makeVisible ( m_Log.countItems ()  - 1);
                    Stop ();
                }
        }
}
```

Listing Four

```
protected Socket m_Socket = null;
protected Connection m_Connection;
protected DataInputStream m_InStream;
protected DataOutputStream m_OutStream;
List m_Log;

public Session ( Socket socket, Connection connection, List Log)
{
    m_Log = Log;
    if(socket != null)
    {
        try
        {
            m_Socket = socket;
            m_OutStream = new DataOutputStream ( m_Socket.getOutputStream());
            m_InStream = new DataInputStream ( m_Socket.getInputStream());
        } catch ( IOException e)
        {
            addLogItem ( "Could not duplicate connection: "+e.getMessage());
        }
        m_Connection = connection;

        start();
    }
    else
    {
        stop();
    }
}
```

Listing Five

```
public void run ()
{
    addLogItem ( "New Session Thread Started");
    while (true)
    {
        if (manageConnection() == false)
            Stop();
    }
}
protected boolean manageConnection()
{
    int minutes = new Date().getMinutes();
```

```
int ID = -1;

try
{
    Date date = new Date();

    if( date.getMinutes() != minutes)
    {
        minutes = date.getMinutes();
        m_OutStream.writeBytes( TrackerData.buildHeartBeat());
    }
    if ( m_InStream.available() > 0)
    {

        byte Stream[] = new byte[m_InStream.available()];
        m_InStream.readFully(Stream);
        String IncomingString = new String(Stream, 0);

        TrackerData TrackerPacket = new TrackerData(IncomingString);
        if( TrackerPacket.parsePacket() )
        {
            switch( TrackerPacket.getType() )
            {
            case TrackerPacket.QUERY:
                ID = getDBItem(TrackerPacket);
                TrackerPacket.setID(ID);

                if(ID != -1)
                {
                    addLogItem("User Queried");
                }
                else
                    addLogItem("User Query Failed");

                sendReply(TrackerPacket, TrackerPacket.UPDATE);
                break;

            case TrackerPacket.SET:
                ID = addDBItem(TrackerPacket);
                TrackerPacket.setID(ID);

                if(ID != -1)
                    addLogItem("New DB Entry");
                else
                    addLogItem("New DB Entry Attemp Failed");
                sendReply(TrackerPacket, TrackerPacket.UPDATE);
                break;
            case TrackerPacket.UPDATE:
                ID = updateDBItem(TrackerPacket);
                TrackerPacket.setID(ID);

                if(ID != -1)
                    addLogItem("DB Entry Update");
                else
```

```
                        addLogItem("DB Entry Update Failed");

                        sendReply(TrackerPacket, TrackerPacket.UPDATE);
                        break;
                }
            }
        }
    } catch (IOException f)
    {
        addLogItem ( f.getMessage());
        return false;
    }
    return true;
}
```

Listing Six

```
protected int addDBItem(TrackerData TrackerPacket)
{
    if((TrackerPacket.getFName().length() < 1) ||
      (TrackerPacket.getLName().length() < 1))
        return -1;
    Statement statement = attachDB();

    if(statement == null)
        return -1;

    String SQLStatement = buildRecordString(TrackerPacket);

    SQLStatement = "INSERT INTO Customers (ContactFirstName,"+
        "ContactLastName, CompanyName, PhoneNumber, Problem, Resolution)"+
        "VALUES " + SQLStatement;
    try
    {
        statement.executeUpdate(SQLStatement);
        statement.close();
    } catch (SQLException e)
    {
        try
        {
            statement.close();
        } catch (SQLException f)
        {
            addLogItem(f.getMessage());
            return -1;
        }
        addLogItem(e.getMessage());
        return -1;
    }
    int ID = getID(TrackerPacket);
    return ID;
}
protected Statement attachDB ()
{
```

```
    try
    {
        Statement statement = m_Connection.createStatement();
        return statement;
    } catch (SQLException e)
    {
        addLogItem ( "Failed to get DB connection: "+e.getMessage() );
        return null;
    }
}
protected String buildRecordString(TrackerData TrackerPacket)
{
    String recordString = new String();
    recordString = "( '"+TrackerPacket.getFName()+"'"+
        ", '"+TrackerPacket.getLName()+"'"+
        ", '"+TrackerPacket.getCompany()+"'"+
        ", '"+TrackerPacket.getPhone()+"'"+
        ", '"+TrackerPacket.getProblem()+"'"+
        ", '"+TrackerPacket.getResolution()+"')";

    return recordString;
}
```

Listing Seven

```
protected int getID( TrackerData TrackerPacket)
{
    int ID = -1;

    Statement statement = attachDB();
    ResultSet rs;

    if(statement == null)
        return ID;
    try
    {
        String SQLStatement = new String();
        SQLStatement = "SELECT * FROM Customers WHERE ContactFirstName = '"
            + TrackerPacket.getFName() + "' AND ContactLastName = '"
            + TrackerPacket.getLName()       + "' AND CompanyName = '"
            + TrackerPacket.getCompany() + "' AND    PhoneNumber = '"
            + TrackerPacket.getPhone() + "' AND Problem = '"
            + TrackerPacket.getProblem()+ "' AND Resolution = '"
            + TrackerPacket.getResolution()+"'";
        rs = statement.executeQuery(SQLStatement);
        rs.next();
        ID = rs.getInt(1);
        rs.close();
        statement.close();
    } catch (SQLException e)
    {
        try
        {
            statement.close();
```

```
        } catch (SQLException f)
        {
            addLogItem(f.getMessage());
        }
        addLogItem(e.getMessage());
    }
    return ID;
}
```

Listing Eight

```
public boolean parsePacket()
{
    if(Packet != null)
    {
        StringTokenizer ParsedPacket = new StringTokenizer(Packet, "-");
        int type;
        int len;

        while(ParsedPacket.hasMoreElements())
        {
            Type = type = getType (ParsedPacket.nextToken());
            switch(type)
            {
            case UPDATE:
            case SET:
                if (type == UPDATE)
                {
                    len = getLength(ParsedPacket.nextToken());
                    setID(Integer.parseInt(getString(ParsedPacket, len)));
                }

                len = getLength(ParsedPacket.nextToken());
                setFName(getString(ParsedPacket, len));

                len = getLength(ParsedPacket.nextToken());
                setLName(getString(ParsedPacket, len));

                len = getLength(ParsedPacket.nextToken());
                setCompany(getString(ParsedPacket, len));

                len = getLength(ParsedPacket.nextToken());
                setPhone(getString(ParsedPacket, len));

                len = getLength(ParsedPacket.nextToken());
                setProblem(getString(ParsedPacket, len));

                len = getLength(ParsedPacket.nextToken());
                setResolution(getString(ParsedPacket,len));
                return true;

            case QUERY:
                len = getLength(ParsedPacket.nextToken());
                setID(Integer.parseInt(getString(ParsedPacket, len)));
```

```
                    return true;

                case HEARTBEAT:
                    len = getLength(ParsedPacket.nextToken());
                    getString(ParsedPacket,len);
                    break;
            }
        }
    }
    return false;
}
```

Listing Nine

```
public String buildPacket(int type)
{
    int FNameLen = FName.length();
    int LNameLen = LName.length();
    int CompanyLen = Company.length();
    int PhoneLen = Phone.length();
    int ProblemLen = Problem.length();
    int ResolutionLen = Resolution.length();

    String newPacket = new String();
    String ids = new String(Integer.toString(ID));

    switch (type)
    {
    case UPDATE:
    case SET:
        if (ID == -1)
        {
            type = SET;
            newPacket = type + "-"+FNameLen+"-"+FName+"-"
                +LNameLen+"-"+LName+"-"
                +CompanyLen+"-"+Company+"-"
                +PhoneLen+"-"+Phone+"-"
                +ProblemLen+"-"+Problem+"-"
                +ResolutionLen+"-"+Resolution;
        }
        else
        {
            type = UPDATE;

            newPacket = type +"-"+ids.length()+"-"+ids+
                "-"+FNameLen+"-"+FName+"-"
                +LNameLen+"-"+LName+"-"
                +CompanyLen+"-"+Company+"-"
                +PhoneLen+"-"+Phone+"-"
                +ProblemLen+"-"+Problem+"-"
                +ResolutionLen+"-"+Resolution;
        }
        break;
    case QUERY:
```

```
        newPacket = type +"-"+ids.length()+"-"+ids;
        break;
    }
    return newPacket;
}
```

End Listings

How Do I Use CORBA from Java?

Cliff Berg

The Common Object Request Broker Architecture (CORBA) is a standard architecture for designing interoperable software components for heterogeneous computing networks. Modules written in various languages can be used together, exchanging objects and method calls across the network without your having to consider the nature of the underlying network or environments. Clearly, CORBA will play a major role in distributed computing.

This month, I'll examine how you can use Java to implement a CORBA application that is representative of the way that CORBA is likely to be used. In doing so, I'll revisit the chat application from my June 1996 column. For more information on CORBA, refer to "Networking Objects with CORBA," by Mark Betz (*Dr. Dobbs Journal*, November 1995); "OMG's CORBA," by Mark Betz (*Dr. Dobb's Special Report on Interoperable Objects*, Winter 1994/95); or *CORBA Fundamentals and Programming*, by Jon Siegel et al. (Wiley, 1996).

Why Use CORBA?

If the chat program worked fine without it, why use CORBA? Recall that, to build the chat program, I had to implement a simple protocol between the client and server: Clients sent characters to the server, then the server echoed

Cliff, vice president of technology of Digital Focus, can be contacted at cliffbdf@digitalfocus.com. To submit questions, check out the Java Developer FAQ Web site at http://www.digitalfocus.com/faq/. Reprinted courtesy of Dr. Dobb's Journal.

those characters to all clients. However, to add features to the chat program—allowing users to identify themselves by name, for example—you would have to build a layered protocol (on top of the data stream) that could contain such control information. Consequently, you would end up writing Java classes to manage that protocol and all of its mechanics.

CORBA does this for you. In a CORBA application, you can concentrate on what methods you want to provide on the client and server, and forget about how you send that information back and forth. CORBA provides a way to create remote objects (on which you can make remote method calls). Further, the resulting protocol is independent of the implementation language, so you can mix components written in Java with components written in C++ and other languages. The interfaces for the components are written in the IDL specification language; CORBA vendors typically provide IDL compilers that generate code in your language of choice. This makes CORBA ideal for integrating new software with legacy systems written in a variety of languages.

Furthermore, Netscape will incorporate the Visigenic CORBA implementation (written in Java) into Navigator. Thus, the most popular browser will contain embedded CORBA classes that can be used in your Java applets, eliminating the time that would normally be required for the browser to download those components.

Choosing a CORBA Provider

Many companies are providing CORBA Java implementations (bindings), including Sun. At the time of this writing, however, Sun's Java implementation is relatively new. In particular, Sun does not yet provide the important IIOP protocol—a sort of lingua franca for CORBA. All CORBA implementations are supposed to provide IIOP. Sun's surely will—it just isn't ready yet (although it may be by the time you read this). Another consideration is that the version you choose should provide full CORBA 2.0 compatibility. This includes the capability for applets to act as servers. You might, at first, think that you would never write an applet that is a server. After all, if you cannot guarantee an applet will be reliably available, how can it ever be a practical server? However, when you start using CORBA, you will find that an applet server is the most effective way to design a system that automatically updates changes in state in client applets. For example, assume there is an update to a database in the midst of a user composing a new transaction; with CORBA, all the server has to do is call a method that executes on the client asynchronously. In this scenario, the client acts as a CORBA server whenever it receives and handles a remote method call from the main "server."

CORBA-fying the Chat Program

Recall that the chat system consists of a server program and multiple chat clients—all communicating. The server serializes the interactions of the chatting clients and provides services (such as user identification and the like).

The first step in designing a CORBA service is to define its call interface—the set of methods that clients of the service will call remotely. Remote method invocation is similar to remote procedure call (RPC), with the additional capability to pass objects around the network and invoke methods in the context of a remote object.

Passing parameters and objects around is known as "marshaling." To marshal, according to the Random House online dictionary, is to "arrange in proper or effective order"—and that is what CORBA does when it marshals our method calls and parameters. It converts them into a stream of bytes that can be sent serially across a network, then unmarshaled at the other end so that the receiving CORBA interface can make sense of the bytes and know what method to call.

Since both the chat client and chat server will be acting as CORBA servers, you need to define two CORBA call interfaces. It is standard practice in CORBA applications to use IDL to define interfaces. Fortunately, IDL is similar to Java. Our chat server (implemented in IDL) contains the methods in Listing One and maps very closely to Java. When you run Listing One through an IDL compiler to generate Java code, the compiler generates a client stub and server skeleton. You don't have to mess with the stub: It is the piece of code that does all of the marshaling for the CORBA client. For example, when the client calls *putLine()*, it is actually calling a method in the generated stub. The stub marshals the method name and parameters into a stream, then sends this to the CORBA server (a program that makes a set of methods available to remote clients), which then unmarshals the stream and, depending on which method name is specified, calls the appropriate method on the server.

The skeleton is the empty set of methods on the server that get called—you must fill in these empty methods with real code. In a typical Java implementation of CORBA, the generated skeleton is an interface, and all you have to do is implement the interface in a class, then create an instance of that class when publishing the service. Our implementation of this interface is called *ChatServerSvcsImpl*.

Clients find the CORBA service because it is registered with an Object Request Broker (ORB) that provides an object identification service. This means that the service has chosen a name for itself and announced that name to the ORB via an *obj_is_ready()* method call. The ORB is an application that

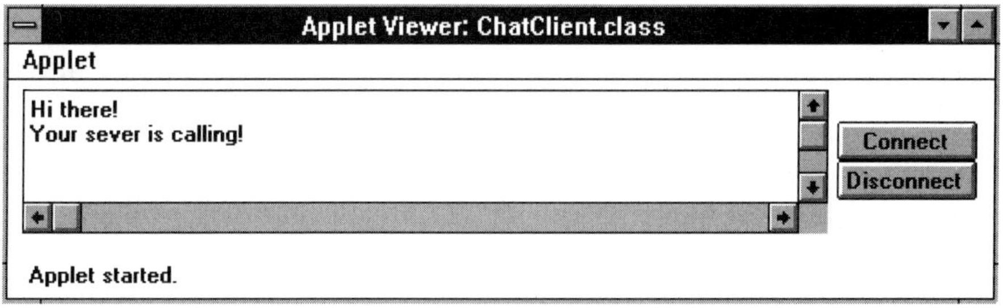

Figure 1: *A CORBA-ized applet.*

is provided by your CORBA vendor and normally runs on the same machine that hosts the Java applet.

Whenever users type a character into the text window on the chat client, the client intercepts the event and, rather than display the character, calls *putc(char)* on the server. The server then goes down its list of clients, telling each client to insert a character at the same position in its client text area. To do this, the server calls a similar method, also called *putc()*, but on each client. The client is acting as a server (because it is providing a method that can be called remotely). Listing Two is the full chat-client interface. The list of methods is shorter because the client does not require methods for registering new clients, and so on.

Since the chat client is also a CORBA server, it will have a stub and a skeleton. In this case, the stub will execute on the chat-server platform, and the skeleton will execute on the chat-client platform. The stub provides the interface for the chat server to call whenever it wants to update a chat client. The skeleton is the chat client's bridge between the CORBA machinery and client's remote-call interface. Our client code has to contain a class that implements the skeleton (just like the chat server). This class is called *ChatClientSvcsImpl*.

The implementation of chat-client methods is straightforward. When *putc()* is called (remotely), the chat client merely appends a character to the user's text area. The *backspace()* method is a little more complicated; see Listing Three.

Since this is a chat application, you do not want users to be able to modify the chat history—they should only be able to append text. Therefore, *backspace()* has to make sure that the client is positioned at the end of the text area. It does this by calling the Java AWT method *TextArea.appendText()* with an empty string as input. This places the insert position at the end of the text area. It then replaces the character at the end with an empty string—effectively deleting the character.

To use these interfaces, you create a *ChatClient* and *ChatServer* class. Our *ChatServer* class is almost trivial. Listing Four, the main routine, performs these calls.

The constant NAME_OF_CHAT_SERVER_SVCS is the string name of the service we want to publish; in our case, we use *ChatServerSvcs*, although it could be anything. The *CORBA.ORB.init()* call initialized the connection to the ORB, and the *BOA_init()* starts the component that allows this program to be a server. *obj_ is_ready()* registers the actual instance of *ChatServerSvcsImpl* servicing the incoming calls—the CORBA skeleton will forward incoming requests to this object; this object must implement the skeleton Java interface generated from the IDL compiler.

The *ChatClient* class is more complex. It starts the ORB link by calling the CORBA *init()* method, then instantiates the text area and a Connect/Disconnect button. I have an *action()* method for handling button events. When users click the Connect button, *action* executes Listing Five.

The first line asks the server to reserve a name for the new client. I would prefer to have the server choose a name as part of the *open()* call, but it cannot because you cannot call *open()* until you have constructed a *ChatClientSvcsImpl* object, and that requires a service name. Since there is a chicken-and-egg problem with getting the name in the *open()* call, I designed the *ChatServerSvcs* to provide the *getUniqueName()* method (to allow the client to determine a unique name for itself, since there will be multiple clients chatting).

After you call *obj_is_ready()*, the client service can accept remote calls. You do not have to call *impl_is_ready()*; this method forces the program to block if it is only listening for requests, because Java will terminate the virtual machine if only daemon threads are running. In the case of the chat client, the user-interface components are running, so you do not have to worry about the program terminating.

Finally, the call to *open()* is a remote call to the *ChatServerSvcs*, which registers the client with the server. It adds the *chatClientSvcs* instance to the server's list of clients. It also associates the *userName* with that instance, in case it needs it later. Figure 1 shows this applet. The complete source code is available on the CD-ROM, and at the Digital Focus site (http://www.digitalfocus.com/ddj/code). The Visigenic Java toolkit is at Visigenic's web site (http://www.visigenic.com).

Other Issues

One difficulty encountered with using a Java CORBA applet from a browser is that the applet may need to access remote objects on multiple servers—but the browser will not allow the applet to open a connection to any machine other than the one it came from. CORBA vendors have solved this problem by building proxy components into their server-side software. These components forward object requests to other machines when needed. Also, some firewalls will not pass the object stream that CORBA protocols require. Some CORBA vendors address this problem by piggybacking the object stream onto the HTTP protocol, to get it past a firewall, then reextracting the stream at the server side.

It would also be nice if it were possible to write only in Java (and not have to use IDL). Visigenic's next release allows you to do this—it generates stubs and skeletons directly from compiled Java interfaces.

Summary

CORBA provides a powerful alternative to CGI. You can write true distributed programs, treating the Internet as one giant operating system. Gone are the days of stuffing parameters into CGI input streams and generating HTML output. A Java client can interact directly with a server-based program using distributed protocols such as CORBA. What's more, the interaction can be bidirectional, making it possible for the server to update the client when changes of state occur, without the client having to poll. The possibilities are limitless. Netscape's decision to bundle a robust Java CORBA facility into its set of built-in Java packages means that there is no overhead in using CORBA-ized Java applets within the Netscape environment. Other Java platforms are expected to follow suit and will soon provide similar embedded CORBA functionality. Regardless, a Java CORBA applet will work in any Java-enabled browser, whether the CORBA functionality is embedded or not. You can expect to see a lot of CORBA from now on.

Listing One

```
interface ChatServerSvcs
{
   string getUniqueName(in string baseName)
         raises (Project::CannotEstablishConnection);
   void open(in string clientName, in ChatClientSvcs cc)
         raises (Project::CannotEstablishConnection);
   void close(in string clientName)
         raises (UnidentifiedUser);
   void putc(in char cin);
   void puts(in string sin);
   void putLine(in string sin);
   void backspace();
   UserList getUsers();
   void identifySelf(in string oldname, in string newname)
         raises (NonUniqueUser, UnidentifiedUser);
};
```

Listing Two

```
interface ChatClientSvcs
{
   void putc(in char cin);

   void puts(in string sin);
   void putLine(in string sin);
   void backspace();
};
```

Listing Three

```
public void backspace()
{
   textArea.appendText("");    // position insert position at the end
   int curpos = textArea.getSelectionStart();
   if (curpos == 0) return;
   textArea.replaceText("", curpos-1, curpos);
}
```

Listing Four

```
orb = CORBA.ORB.init();
boa = orb.BOA_init();
```

```
chatServerSvcs = new ChatServerSvcsImpl(NAME_OF_CHAT_SERVER_SVCS);
boa.obj_is_ready(chatServerSvcs);
boa.impl_is_ready();
```

Listing Five

```
userName = chatServerSvcs.getUniqueName(BASE_NAME_OF_CHAT_CLIENT_SVCS + ".");
boa = orb.BOA_init();
chatClientSvcs = new ChatClientSvcsImpl(userName, textArea);
boa.obj_is_ready(chatClientSvcs);
chatServerSvcs.open(userName, chatClientSvcs);
```

End Listings

Tuning Java Performance

Paul Tyma

Although the Java programming language has opened up new dimensions in the world of programming, it's also uncovered some new challenges. Given that Java is platform independent and interpreted, writing code that performs well is no longer cut-and-dried. Java programmers need to focus their optimization efforts on a higher level, independent of architectural idiosyncrasies.

In this article, I'll examine how compiled Java runs, then present techniques for speeding things up. The coding guidelines I'll present will perform well on any platform. As always, your first consideration in getting the best performance out of your code should be your choice of algorithms and data structures. Binary searches, quick sorts, and hash tables offer great benefits in the right situations.

The data in this article was recorded from running Java on several different machines. The optimizations I discuss do not assume any platform-specific features. For the most part, these are well-published techniques, but focused for Java.

Paul, who is a PhD candidate in computer engineering at Syracuse University, is president of preEmptive Solutions, an Internet technologies company. He can be reached at ptyma@preemptive.com. Reprinted courtesy of Dr. Dobb's Journal.

What to Optimize?

Your greatest performance gains will come from speeding up the most-used code, such as highly iterated loops and popularly called methods. Focusing optimization on these areas will give you the best gain-for-effort ratio.

One of Java's greatest selling points is its architectural independence, which it accomplishes by compiling its code into its own intermediate representation, not any specific machine language. Though it's typical for compilers to generate intermediate code and then create actual machine code, Java doesn't go that far. Instead, it leaves its executable in this intermediate form.

Java's intermediate representation is made up of instructions termed "byte-codes." The individual bytecodes look much like the assembly language of *any* given machine. The intermediate representation (and, subsequently, the Java virtual machine) is designed as a stack-based architecture. Most people who know the assembly language of a modern machine are used to register-based machines. In a stack-based machine, there are no registers. There is a stack where you can push, pop, and manipulate data, but that is the extent of the design.

Another point to consider in deciding where to optimize is that Java byte-codes are currently interpreted. The future promises dynamic ("just-in-time") compilers that jump in just as a Java program is executed to compile the byte-codes into the target machine code. The final result is that the Java program is running the same as any other compiled program (with a short pause at the start while the dynamic compiler works its magic). Unfortunately, these compilers might not be widely available for a long time. So for now, you're forced to live with interpretation.

A significant portion of interpretation time is spent dealing with overhead. Instruction execution requires the following steps:

- Fetch the instruction.
- Decode the instruction.
- Fetch the arguments of the instruction.
- Execute the instruction.

These steps are there whether it's a CPU executing its machine code or the Java interpreter executing its bytecodes. The difference is that in an interpreter, the first three steps are overhead. For a CPU executing machine code, much of the work of the first three steps is soaked up in the pipe of modern superscalar processors.

There is no real way of removing this overhead for each instruction, short of dynamic compilation. Because of Java's architectural independence, we can't rely on the performance tricks of any given architecture. You don't know if the target processor has an on-chip cache, what its jump-prediction algorithms are, or anything else. Even the CISC concept of expensive versus inexpensive instructions doesn't carry over very well: Interpretation tends to smooth over individual instruction costs. Given these uncertainties, the best solution is to simply reduce the total number of instructions that are executed.

This doesn't necessarily mean to reduce the size of your code. Small bits of code can certainly loop themselves into painfully slow performance, but we're more interested in decreasing the number of executed instructions wherever possible—while still achieving the desired output. All this talk has been at the level of interpreters, but don't fret—even when dynamic compilation comes around, it too will benefit from fewer instructions to compile and run.

Many general programming-language optimization rules apply to Java. The *int* data type is faster than *long* (as is *float* compared to *double*). A *long* is twice the size of an *int*, making accesses comparably slower. In addition, Java's *int* data type is already bigger than some programmers are used to (it is 32 bit, whereas 16 bit is common for many PC C compilers). So, wherever you can, keep things down to *int* and *float*.

In general, iterative code is faster than equivalent recursive code. This is true in any language, since method calls are expensive.

Use the Best Algorithm, Use the Best Data Structure

The class file (bytecodes) that results from compiling Java programs is amazingly small. Even intensive graphical programs will often be only a few kilobytes, because accesses to Java's API library rely on finding the classes on the machine executing the program. For example, drawing a line actually calls code in the java/classes directory. Unfortunately, calls to system functions (drawing graphics, opening files, and the like) are largely a crapshoot. Often when optimizing, you are (transparently) leaving the beautiful, architecture-independent world of Java and implicitly executing native code. For our interests, it's important to note that you can't count on the speed of such operations for different architectures. Drawing a line may be swift on some machines but a painful operation on others. In general, performance of code that is heavily dependent upon API calls is largely out of your hands.

Squeezing performance out of object-oriented languages has never been easy. For one thing, object-oriented programming encourages reusable classes. From a grand code-development standpoint, the ability to reuse code for future projects increases long-term programmer productivity. However, generic classes usually require many conditional statements to support a relatively generic set of input. This level of support increases code size and costs processing time.

Consider Java's prebuilt *stack* class. This class accepts *any* object to be pushed on the stack. Certainly, that encompasses a broad usage. However, often you only need to stack something as mundane as integers. The built-in stack class will do this—at least after you perform conversions of your integers to and from object status. To achieve better performance, you would be better off creating a stack class specifically designed to stack integers.

Inlining

Inlining is everybody's favorite optimization technique, and for good reason—performance gains can be dramatic. Good program design usually involves relatively fine-grained modularity. With increasing numbers of discrete methods comes increasing numbers of method calls. From a readability and design standpoint, that's great: Discrete tasks in a class are logically placed in their own methods. Unfortunately, from a performance standpoint, method calls are expensive. Depending upon the implementation, this involves saving the current state, performing a jump (which may entail moving to currently uncached memory), and keeping track of where to return.

Again, interpreted environments are hit with extra instructions that don't actually work towards performing the goal of the program but instead deal with overhead. Object-oriented programming often exacerbates the problem by providing countless accessor methods within a class to get (effective) read-only access to its private variables. Accessor methods are nothing more than a variable access (a theoretical single memory read) but still incur all the calling overhead. To overcome this problem, compilers often attempt to inline methods—in effect, placing the method body at the call site and ignoring any semblance of an actual subroutine call. Listing One is part of a class intended to store and manipulate matrices.

The *tester* class creates two *matrix_work* objects and multiplies them together. The size of the matrices are substantial to expose the effect of optimizations. The A.multiply(B) statement took several seconds on all tested

```
public final int getrows() {
        return rows;  }
public final int getcols() {
        return cols;  }
public final int getcoord(int r,
int c) { return matrix[r][c]; }
```

Example 1: *Inlining accessor methods.*

```
class banking {

   synchronized public void deposit_checking() {...}
   synchronized public void withdraw_checking() {...}
   synchronized public void deposit_savings() {...}
   synchronized public void withdraw_savings() {...}
   }

// instantiated elsewhere with
   banking myMoney = new banking();

// multiple threads can now access myMoney
   .
   .
```

Example 2: *Ensuring data integrity.*

machines. For future comparisons, I'll use the relative run time of 5000 milliseconds.

To have the javac compiler perform method inlining requires two steps. First, it will only inline static, private, or final methods. You won't always be able to ensure inlining—that is, a private accessor method is only so useful. Secondly, you need to specify the –O option when compiling. After testing (and debugging) is done, there is rarely a good reason not to compile your classes with this option. For Listing One, I inlined the three accessor methods by making them final, as in Example 1. This brought the run time from 5000 milliseconds to approximately 3500. Across all architectures tested, the savings was at least 25 percent. Considering that adding the final modifier to these statements is a trivial act, it's certainly worth the effort. The change in the bytecode generated was evident, as a comparison between Listing Two and Listing Three shows. The only change is from a method invocation to a *getfield* (that is, an instance variable access).

Declaring methods as static or private also allows inlining where applicable. According to post-inlined bytecodes, the A object is accessing private variables of the B object. The compiler runs its checks and ensures that your code does not violate any access restrictions. After that, it takes whatever liberties it can to create faster code. To put it another way, once the compiler is sure you've followed the rules, it knows where it can safely break them.

You can also inline values by declaring variables as final. In general, this is analogous to utilizing the preprocessor in C to replace some string by a value (specified via the *#define* macro). This technique improves readability, maintainability, and saves a memory access at run time.

Synchronized Methods

Synchronization of methods is applicable when using multithreading, and it is effectively how Java utilizes the operating-system concept of monitors.

```
class banking {

    Object banking = new Object();
    Object checking = new Object();

    public void depositChecking() {
        synchronized(checking) {...}}
    public void withdrawChecking() {
        synchronized(checking) {...}}
    public void depositSavings() {
        synchronized(savings) {...}}
    public void withdrawSavings() {
        synchronized(savings) {...}}
    }
```

Example 3: *Modified version Example 2.*

Declaring a method as synchronized requires the method to obtain a lock before it is permitted to execute. If another method currently has that lock, the first must wait for the lock until it is available.

This level of synchronization is key in assuring the protection of critical sections of code. However, it is important to remember that every object and every class has exactly one lock. Therefore, if a thread has the lock for a given object, then no other thread may enter any of the synchronized methods within that object. If a thread must needlessly wait for a lock, you may want to redesign your class. To ensure data integrity in Example 2, it is important that not more than one thread is accessing any one account at a time. Logically, there is no reason one thread can't deposit into checking while another thread is withdrawing from savings (assuming these are separate accounts). With the aforementioned code, for a given banking object, that is not possible. The problem is that as soon as any thread enters one of the methods, it obtains a lock for the entire *myMoney* object, generating an unnecessary performance hit.

There are several solutions to this dilemma. First, consider whether the class is designed with logical contents. For the aforementioned example, it would likely have made more sense to have two separate classes, a savings account class and a checking account class. Another solution would be to not declare methods as synchronized. Protection of critical sections is vital, but overuse hits performance and increases the chance of deadlock.

Besides the possibility of uselessly blocking a thread, the overhead generated by synchronizing a method is significant. Tests have shown that a noninlined, unsynchronized accessor method can run four times faster than a synchronized one. In addition to slowing running time, declaring a method as synchronized removes the compiler's ability to inline that method.

To bring synchronization down to a finer level, you can specify objects to be used as synchronization objects. Example 3 is a slightly modified version of the code in Example 2. The synchronizations do not lock the *myMoney* object; they lock the checking and banking objects. Again, it would be more desirable to split this type of class in two. However, in some situations that may not be possible and the use of synchronization objects can be useful.

```
(a) for (g=0;g<value-2;++g) {
        x[g] = g*2;
    }


(b) int temp = value-2;
    for (g=0;g<temp;++g) {
        x[g] = g*2;
    }
```

Example 4: *(a) The JDK Beta 2.0 version of the compiler does not support code motion; (b) using a temporary variable to improve performance.*

Code Motion

The JDK Beta 2.0 version of the compiler surprisingly did not support code motion; see Example 4(a).

Many contemporary compilers realize the value-2 expression has no dependencies within the loop. Therefore, a compiler could calculate value-2 prior to loop execution and use the result in the conditional with *g* (as a temporary variable). Unfortunately, in the javac compiler, the expression value-2 is calculated for each iteration of the loop even though the result is the same every time. In Example 4(a), the effect is not very detrimental. But it should be obvious that complex operations in that situation could needlessly waste processing time. Eliminating this type of transgression is nearly free and can be done with a temporary variable; see Example 4(b).

The practice of eliminating redundant calculations can be applied to array indexing. Every time you access an array, the system must determine the indexed memory location—that is, an implicit calculation. On top of that, Java's VM does array range checking. Although run-time array bounds checking has become a well-optimized science, its cost can still be noticeable. Wherever you can, eliminate redundant array references. Looking back to Listing One, there are a significant number of redundant array index calculations embedded in the multiply method. Listing Four shows a new *multiply* method exhibiting (somewhat overzealous) array index calculation movement.

The *temprow* vector is assigned to a row of the matrix array. For all processing past this point, the code will be interested only in one row of matrix, so pointing to the row directly will save having to follow the row pointer each time. Additionally, a temporary variable is used to accumulate the values and is assigned to the *T* array location after the loop. This way, calculating the index into *T* is done only once instead of for each iteration of the *k* loop (*i* and *j* do not change inside the *k* loop).

Recall that inlining the accessor methods brought the run time down from a relative value of 5000 milliseconds to approximately 3500. Implementation of the code change in Listing Four brought the run time down to 2400 milliseconds. Inlining and code motion (array index calculation motion, to be specific) reduced run time by over 50 percent. As a parting triviality, you'll also notice that the loop variable declarations (variables *i*, *j*, and *k*) were moved. The Java VM peculiarly treats the first three local variables of a method (parameters are counted first) slightly differently than all subsequent ones. Several bytecode instructions are tailored specifically for the first three locals, providing a tiny performance improvement (a 2 percent speed increase was measured for Listing Four).

Conclusion

Given Java's close relationship to C, many of the same high-level optimizations pay off. Java's architecture neutrality forbids using CPU tricks to speed up code. No assumptions are allowed. Subsequent generations of Java compilers and interpreters (and dynamic compilers) are likely to improve performance all on their own. Java code that relies heavily on system-dependent API calls are destined to be unpredictable. Good object-oriented design and performance coding have always had their conflicts. This is not to say that good design can't be fast—it just takes a smart programmer and compiler.

Listing One

```
/*============ Matrix Work class ==============*/
 class matrix_work {
    private int matrix[][];
    private int rows,cols;
    matrix_work(int r, int c) {
        rows = r;
        cols = c;
        matrix = new int[rows][cols];
        populate();


    }
    public int getrows() { return rows; }
    public int getcols() { return cols; }
    public int getcoord(int r, int c) { return matrix[r][c]; }
/* Matrix multiplication - returns number of elements in new matrix */
    public int multiply(matrix_work B) {

        if (cols != B.getrows()) throw new badMultException();

        int numels = rows * B.getcols();
        int T[][] = new int[rows][B.getcols()];
        int i,j,k;

        for (i=0;i<rows;++i) {
          for (j=0;j<B.getcols();++j) {
            T[i][j] = 0;
            for (k=0;k<cols;++k) {
          T[i][j] += matrix[i][k] * B.getcoord(k,j);
          }
           }
          }
        matrix = T;
        cols = B.getcols();
        return numels;
        }

/* Populates the matrix */
    public void populate() { ..enlightening population code here }
/* ============= Testing class =========== */
    class tester {
    public static void main (String args[]) {
        matrix_work A = new matrix_work(80,40);
        matrix_work B = new matrix_work(40,65);
        int numels = A.multiply(B);
        }
    }
```

Listing Two

```
Method int getcols()
   0 aload_0
   1 getfield #19 <Field matrix_work.cols I>
   4 ireturn
     .
     .
     .
  90 iinc 5 1
  93 iload 5
  95 aload_1

  96 invokevirtual #20 <Method matrix_work.getcols()I>
  99 if_icmplt 35
     .
     .
     .
```

Listing Three

```
Method int getcols()
   0 aload_0
   1 getfield #13 <Field matrix_work.cols I>
   4 ireturn
     .
     .
     .
  92 iinc 5 1

  95 iload 5
  97 aload_1
  98 getfield #13 <Field matrix_work.cols I>
 101 if_icmplt 35
     .
     .
     .
```

Listing Four

```
public final int multiply(matrix_work B) {
  if (cols != B.getrows()) throw new badMultException();

  int j,k,i;
  int numels = rows * B.getcols();
  int T[][] = new int[rows][B.getcols()];

  int temp,temprow[];
  for (i=0;i<rows;++i) {
    temprow = matrix[i];
    for (j=0;j<B.getcols();++j) {
      temp = 0;
      for (k=0;k<cols;++k) {
```

```
      temp += temprow[k] * B.getcoord(k,j);
      }
    T[i][j] = temp;
    }
  }
matrix = T;
cols = B.getcols();
return numels;
}
```

End Listings

How Garbage Collection Can Increase Speed

Bruce Eckel

In the October, 1996 issue of *Web Techniques*, I spent most of my column explaining why Java couldn't possibly be as fast or faster than C++. Recently, while speaking at the Visual J++ Developer's Conference in Europe, I met Ian Ellison-Taylor, a developer from Microsoft's Java-development team, and Mike Toutonghi, who wrote significant parts of the Microsoft JVM. They patiently explained how Microsoft had implemented Java, and I began to see that much of my perspective stemmed from Sun's inefficient implementation, so there was no model to show how fast Java can be. All I had heard was Sun, saying "Java can be really great," and that wears thin after a while.

Part of my misunderstanding came from being cloistered with the C++ model for too long. C++ is focused on everything happening statically, at compile time, so that the runtime image of the program is very small and fast.

Bruce is the author of Thinking in Java *(freely available at http://www.EckelObjects.com/Eckel),* Thinking in C++ *(Prentice-Hall, 1995), and* C++ Inside & Out *(Osborne/McGraw-Hill, 1993). He's published over 100 articles in numerous magazines, participates on the ANSI/ISO C++ committee, speaks regularly at conferences, and is the C++ and Java track chair for the Software Development conference. He provides public and private seminars and design consulting in C++ and Java. Reprinted courtesy of* Web Techniques.

C++ is also based heavily on the C model, primarily for backward compatibility, but sometimes simply because it worked a particular way in C so it was the easiest approach in C++. One of the most important cases is the way memory is managed in C and C++. This has to do with one of my more fundamental assertions about Java's slow speed: In Java, all objects must be created on the heap.

Allocating Objects

In C++, creating objects on the stack is fast because when you enter a particular scope the stack pointer is moved down once to allocate storage for all the stack-based objects created in that scope. When you leave the scope (after all the local destructors have been called) the stack pointer is moved up once. Creating heap objects in C++ is typically much slower because it's based on the C concept of a heap as a big pool of memory that must be recycled. When you call *delete* in C++, the released memory leaves a hole in the heap. Therefore, when you call *new*, the storage-allocation mechanism must try to fit the storage for your object into any existing holes; otherwise you'll rapidly run out of heap storage. Searching for available pieces of memory is why allocating heap storage has such a performance impact in C++; it's far faster to create stack-based objects.

Again, this makes sense because so much of C++ is based on doing everything at compile time. But in Java things happen more dynamically in certain places, and this changes the model. For example, the garbage collector can have a significant impact on the speed of object creation. Storage release affecting storage allocation may seem odd, but that's the way Microsoft's JVM works, so allocating storage for heap objects in Java can be nearly as fast as creating storage on the stack in C++.

Think of the C++ heap (and a slow implementation of a Java heap) as a yard where each object stakes out its own piece of turf. This real estate can become available later, and must be reused. In Microsoft's JVM, the Java heap is quite different; it's more like a conveyor belt that moves forward every time you allocate a new object, making object-storage allocation remarkably rapid. The "heap pointer" is simply moved forward into virgin territory, so it's effectively the same as C++'s stack allocation. Bookkeeping creates a little extra overhead, but it's nothing like searching for storage.

You might observe that the heap isn't a conveyor belt, and if you treat it that way you'll eventually start paging a lot of memory (which means a big performance hit) and run out. But the trick is that the Microsoft JVM garbage collector compacts all the objects in the heap, so you effectively move the "heap pointer" closer to the beginning of the conveyor belt and further away from a page fault. The garbage collector lets you use this high-speed, infinite-free-heap model for allocating storage.

Garbage-Collection Schemes

To understand how this works, you need to understand how the different garbage-collector (GC) schemes work. A simple but very slow GC technique is reference counting, whereby each object contains a reference counter, and every time a handle is attached to an object, the reference count increases. When a handle goes out of scope or is set to *null*, the reference count decreases. Managing reference counts is then a small but constant overhead throughout the lifetime of your program. The garbage collector moves through the objects, and releases storage when it finds one with a reference count of zero. However, if objects circularly refer to each other, they can have nonzero reference counts while still being garbage. Locating such self-referential groups means significant extra work for the garbage collector. Reference counting is commonly used to explain one kind of garbage collection, but isn't part of any JVM implementations.

Microsoft's garbage collection is based not on reference counting but on the idea that any nondead object must ultimately be traceable back to a handle either on the stack or in static storage. The chain may go through several layers of objects, so if you start in the stack and the static storage area and walk through all the handles, you'll find all the live objects throughout the entire web. Detached, self-referential groups are not a problem—they are simply not found, and are therefore automatically garbage.

Microsoft's JVM uses an adaptive garbage-collection scheme with several variants, one of which is "stop-and-copy." The program is stopped, and each live object that is found is copied from one heap to another, leaving behind all the garbage. Objects copied into the new heap are packed end-to-end, compacting the heap and allowing new storage to simply be reeled off the end.

Of course, when an object is moved, its handles must be changed; the handle that comes from tracing the object from the heap or the static storage area can be changed right away. Other handles pointing to this object may be encountered and fixed later during the "walk" (you can imagine a hash table mapping old addresses to new ones).

Two issues make copy collectors inefficient. The first is the idea that you have two heaps between which you slosh all the memory, meaning you must maintain twice as much memory as you need. Microsoft's JVM deals with this by allocating the heap in chunks as needed and simply copying from one chunk to another.

Another garbage-collection variant is "mark-and-sweep." Once your program becomes stable, it may generate little or no garbage. Still, a copy collector wastefully copies all the memory from one place to another. To prevent this, Microsoft's JVM detects that no new garbage is being generated and switches to "mark-and-sweep." For general use, mark and sweep is fairly slow, but when you know you're generating little or no garbage, it's very fast.

Mark-and-sweep also starts from the stack and static storage and traces through all the handles to find live objects. Each time it finds a live object, it sets a flag in it but does not collect it. Only when this marking process is finished does the sweep occur, releasing the dead objects. Because no copying happens, the collector can compact a fragmented heap only by shuffling objects around.

Sun's JVM uses mark-and-sweep all the time. The Sun literature contains many theoretical references to garbage collection as a low-priority, background process. In practice, the Sun garbage collector is run when memory gets low. In addition, mark-and-sweep requires that the program be stopped.

Generation Counting

Since the Microsoft JVM allocates memory in big blocks, a large object gets its own block. Strict stop-and-copy eats up memory by requiring that you copy every live object from the source heap to a new heap before you free it. With blocks, the GC can typically use dead blocks to copy objects to as it collects. Each block has a generation count to keep track of whether it's alive or not. Normally, only the blocks created since the last GC are compacted; all others just get their generation count bumped if they have been referenced from somewhere. This handles short-lived temporary objects. Periodically, a full sweep is made—large objects are still not copied, but blocks containing small objects are copied and compacted. The JVM monitors the efficiency of GC, and if objects are long-lived, it saves time by switching to mark-and-sweep. Similarly, if the heap starts to become fragmented, it switches back to stop-and-copy. So you end up with a mouthful: "adaptive generational stop-and-copy mark-and-sweep."

Other Speedups

Another speedup in Microsoft's JVM involves the operation of the loader and Just-In-Time (JIT) compiler. When a class must be loaded (typically, to first create an object of that class), the *.class* file is located and the byte codes are brought into memory. At this point, you can simply JIT all the code, but this has two drawbacks: It takes a little more time that, compounded throughout the life of the program, can add up, and it increases the size of the executable (byte codes are significantly more compact than expanded JIT code). This may cause paging, which definitely slows down a program. The Microsoft approach is "lazy evaluation"—the code is not JIT compiled until necessary, so code that isn't executed may never get JIT compiled.

Because JVMs are external to browsers, you might expect to benefit from the speedups of Microsoft's JVM in Netscape Navigator. Unfortunately, JVMs don't currently interoperate with different browsers—you must either use Microsoft Internet Explorer 3.0 or run standalone Java applications.

At Full Speed

With the combination of its JIT compiler and garbage-collection technology, Microsoft has put a great deal of effort into making Java run as fast as possible; fast enough, it seems, to give C++ some heady competition. But the reason speed was so important to Microsoft is COM: If Java is fast enough, it won't matter what tool—including Java—you use to create your COM objects.

Index